THE REAL DON JUAN

First published in 1990 by Absolute Classics, an imprint of
Absolute Press, 14 Widcombe Crescent, Bath, England

Cover and text design: Ian Middleton

Photoset and printed by The Longdunn Press Ltd, Bristol

ISBN 0 948230 36 3

THE REAL DON JUAN

José Zorrilla

Translated and adapted by Ranjit Bolt

a b s o l u t e   c l a s s i c s

IN MEMORY OF CHRISTOPHER CHETWOOD

FOREWORD

A few months ago, when I was still working as an investment advisor, I got a call from John Retallack of the Oxford Stage Company. He said he had seen the Old Vic production of THE LIAR, and would I like to try my hand at José Zorrilla's DON JUAN TENORIO (which was apparently one of the most popular plays in the Spanish speaking world, although virtually unknown elsewhere). I was cagey at first. There were two basic problems. The first was that I imagined the play was probably in prose (since 19th Century plays tend to be in prose) whereas verse was my forte (if I *had* a forte). Secondly, and more importantly, I guessed the play must be in Spanish (since people called José, in whatever century, have tended to write in Spanish) whereas I myself did not know any Spanish.

Half an hour later there was a message on my desk: "John Retalic (Retaluck?) called – says play in verse." I called John to accept the commission – then went straight to Grant & Cutler, bought a copy and began work that evening. Unfortunately I had omitted to purchase a Spanish dictionary, which must be an essential for anyone translating from the Spanish – let alone someone who doesn't *know* any Spanish. Two days later, now equipped with such a dictionary, I started again and found (hardly surprisingly) that I had completely mis-translated the first eight lines, which was as far as I had got, muddling through on a mixture of Latin and Italian. But thereafter (and with occasional recourse to a rather plodding crib) I never looked back. The extraordinary energy and versatility of Zorrilla's verse – by turns rough-hewn and elegant, hard-bitten and sentimental (all things, in short, to all men) (not to mention his raw sense of theatre, and my own excitement at discovering both a new play and a new language) simply swept me along.

I would not claim for one minute that this is an entirely "Faithful" translation – still less an accurate one – but I hope that some of that variegated and spontaneous quality has come through. It is said that Zorrilla never made much money from writing, but always maintained that were he to stand outside the theatre after a performance of DON JUAN, any one of the departing spectators would have given him the price of a meal. I only wish the man were alive now, so that I could take him out to the best restaurant in town, apologise for my own slips, and try to glean something of how it was all done.

RANJIT BOLT

THE REAL DON JUAN is to be given its première by the Oxford Stage Company in its autumn tour in 1990. The cast is as follows:

DON JUAN TENORIO	JOHN MICHIE
DONA INES	DENISE THOMAS
DON LUIS	DAVID SOLOMON
DON GONZALO DE ULLOA	TERRY MCGINITY
AVELLENADA	TONY CREAN
BUTTARELLI/BRIGIDA	NELLA MARIN
CIUTTI/PORTER/SCULPTOR	WILLIAM LAWRANCE
CENTELLAS	DEREK RIDDELL
DON DIEGO/PASCUAL	RICHARD HENRY
ABBESS/DONA ANA/LUCIA	CARLA MENDONÇA
DIRECTOR	JOHN RETALLACK
DESIGNER	KENNY MILLER
LIGHTING DESIGNER	KEVIN SLEEP
COMPOSER/MUSICAL DIRECTOR	HOWARD GOODALL
FLAMENCO GUITAR MUSIC	JOANNE SPEECHLEY
FIGHT DIRECTOR	JOHN WALLER
CHOREOGRAPHY	SEETA INDRANI

CHARACTERS

DON JUAN TENORIO

DON LUIS MEJIA (A hidalgo)

DON GONZALO DE ULLOA (Commander of the Order of Calatrava)

DON DIEGO TENORIO (Don Juan's father)

DONA INES DE ULLOA (Don Gonzalo's daughter)

DONA ANA DE PANTOJA (Betrothed to Don Luis)

CRISTOFANO BUTTARELLI (Landlord of The Laurel Inn)

CIUTTI (Don Juan's servant)

BRIGIDA (Dona Ines' nurse)

PASCUAL (Servant in the Pantoja household)

CENTELLAS (A Captain, and friend of Don Juan)

AVELLANEDA (A hidalgo, and friend of Centellas and Don Luis)

LUCIA (Dona Ana's maid)

ABBESS (Of the nuns of Calatrava)

PORTER (Of the nuns of Calatrava)

GASTON (Don Luis' servant)

MIGUEL (Butarelli's servant)

MASKERS, ONLOOKERS, CONSTABLES, SOLDIERS, CHERUBS, SPECTRES, SKELETONS

NB: Mejía, Inés, Brígida, Cristófano, Gastón and Lucía are all written with accents. However, for the purposes of this text, Ines should be treated as something of a metrical chameleon – sometimes the Spanish iamb, sometimes the Byronic trochee. I have also taken a liberty with Brigida in one place.

PART ONE

ACT ONE

SCANDAL AND DEBAUCHERY

Cristofano Buttarelli's inn. Door to street, down stage. Tables, jugs, other utensils. Don Juan, masked, sits at a table writing with an enormous quill pen; Buttarelli and Ciutti wait to one side. As the curtain goes up sundry Maskers, Students and Citizens pass through the street door with torches, musical instruments, etc.

DON JUAN: To hell with them and their "festivities" –
I'll shut them up when I've completed this.

BUTTARELLI: Good carnival.

CIUTTI: Good harvest for your till.

BUTTARELLI: This is the silly season in Seville –
Nothing but small fry come to inns like these;
The upper classes are so hard to please –
The rabble, too, at times.

CIUTTI: But not today.

BUTTARELLI: It's true, I've done some damn good business.

CIUTTI: Hey!
Don't talk so loud – you'll get him riled.

He indicates Don Juan.

BUTTARELLI: Is he
Your master?

CIUTTI: Has been for a year.

BUTTARELLI: I see.
And what's he like to work for?

CIUTTI: The best yet:
It's heaven – everything I want I get:
Wine, women, song, unlimited free time –
And all at his expense.

BUTTARELLI: It sounds sublime.
Rich, is he?

CIUTTI: Spends at a horrendous rate.

BUTTARELLI: And honest?

CIUTTI: As an undergraduate!

BUTTARELLI: Noble?

CIUTTI: A prince.

BUTTARELLI: And brave?

CIUTTI: A buccaneer.

BUTTARELLI: Spanish?

CIUTTI: Of course.

BUTTARELLI: His name?

CIUTTI: I've no idea.

BUTTARELLI: I'll bet! Writing a novel is he, then?

CIUTTI: A letter. As the saying goes: "Big pen . . ."

BUTTARELLI: Who to?

CIUTTI: His father.

BUTTARELLI: Well! That's what I call
A son!

CIUTTI: He's an example to us all.

Don Juan signs and folds the letter.

DON JUAN: Ciutti!

CIUTTI: Senor?

DON JUAN: Deliver this epistle
To Ines' nurse – she'll slip it in that missal

I gave her – she's in league with me, you see.
She's promised to supply you with a key –
Bring it back here at once.

CIUTTI: Immediately.

Exit.

DON JUAN: Cristofano!

BUTTARELLI: Signore?

DON JUAN: Vieni qua.

(Buttarelli goes over to him.)

Senti.

BUTTARELLI: Sento.

(Pause as Juan searches for his Italian.)

                              I speak Castilian . . .

DON JUAN: Ah!
Well then, has Don Luis Mejia shown
His face today?

BUTTARELLI: His face is not in town,
And nor's the rest of him.

DON JUAN: You've had no word?

BUTTARELLI: Well, now you come to mention it, I've heard
A story . . .

DON JUAN: Really? Will it shed some light
On matters?

BUTTARELLI: *(Distracted)* Matters? I suppose it might.

DON JUAN: Out with it, then.

BUTTARELLI: *(As before, soliloquising.)* The year is up tonight!
I'd clean forgotten! Have I counted wrong. . . ?

DON JUAN: God, man! Do all your stories take this long?

BUTTARELLI: I'm sorry – I was trying to remember
The details . . .

DON JUAN: Quick! Before I lose my temper . . .

BUTTARELLI: Apparently, this Don Luis Mejia
            Hit on the most ridiculous idea . . .

DON JUAN: The wager? That's an ancient story.

BUTTARELLI: *(Deflated)* Oh.

DON JUAN: Mejia bet Don Juan Tenorio
            That in a given year (such was his whim)
            He'd do more harm, more easily, than him.

BUTTARELLI: You've heard it then.

DON JUAN: I'm totally *au fait* –
            That's why I asked if he'd been here today.

BUTTARELLI: It'd be really something, in my view,
            If they could settle this the way they do
            Their bills.

DON JUAN: Are you implying there's some doubt?
            Mejia might consider backing out?

BUTTARELLI: There's been no sign of either of them yet –
            They've both forgotten all about that bet.

DON JUAN: Enough. Here's gold for you.

            *He hands him two gold coins. Buttarelli bows
            obsequiously.*

BUTTARELLI: Excellency!

            (Pause as he pockets it.)
            Do you know something I don't?

DON JUAN: Possibly.

BUTTARELLI: You think they're coming?

DON JUAN: One is guaranteed.
            But if they both turn up you're going to need
            Two bottles of your finest wine. Good day.

            *Exit Don Juan. Buttarelli watches him go, then
            addresses the audience, rubbing his hands in
            anticipation.*

BUTTARELLI: They're going to keep the bet! They're on their way!
            He's been informed.
            (Noises off.)

What's going on out there?
(He goes to the door.)
It's him again! He's fighting in the square!
It's twenty onto one . . . they're falling back!
They're on the run! And *he's* on the attack!
My God! That pair have reached Castille, alright,
And trouble's on the menu for tonight.
Miguel!

Enter Miguel.

MIGUEL: You called, sir?

BUTTARELLI: See that table there?
I want it laid – our finest silverware –
And fetch two bottles up, the best we've got.

MIGUEL: The Lachrimae?

BUTTARELLI: The Lachrimae – why not?

Miguel goes out as Don Gonzalo enters.

GONZALO: Good evening.

BUTTARELLI: *(Impatient)* What d'you want?

GONZALO: Who owns this place?

BUTTARELLI: You're talking to him now.

GONZALO: Well, in that case.
What do you make of this?

Tosses him a gold coin.

BUTTARELLI: It's gold, of course.

GONZALO: Answer some simple questions and it's yours.

Another obsequious bow from Buttarelli.

BUTTARELLI: Excellency!

GONZALO: Don Juan Tenorio –
D'you know him?

BUTTARELLI: Certainly.

GONZALO: And would you know
Whether he's meeting someone here tonight?

BUTTARELLI: You're Don Luis Mejia, then?

GONZALO: Not quite –
Although I'd like to see their interview.

BUTTARELLI: This table's theirs. Will that one do for you?
It'll be well worth watching.

GONZALO: I dare say.

BUTTARELLI: There aren't two finer men in Spain today.

GONZALO: Viler, you mean.

BUTTARELLI: *(Dismissive)* If any mischief's done
They're sure to be accused by everyone –
It's idle gossip. Let them rape and kill –
Why should I worry, if they pay the bill?
I'm here to tell you . . .

GONZALO: *(Dry)* Quite. It's plain to see
That you're a man of some integrity –
How can I watch them, then, without being seen?
From an adjoining room? Behind a screen?

BUTTARELLI: A mask should do the trick: it's no disgrace,
During a carnival, to hide one's face.
(Gonzalo seems sceptical.)
The contents of a pie we take on trust –
We can't be sure until we cut the crust;
Now, hide your features with a mask or visor –
Until you take it off . . .

GONZALO: . . . we're none the wiser?

BUTTARELLI: Exactly.

GONZALO: Have you one?

BUTTARELLI: I'll go and get it.

    Goes.

GONZALO: Such total wickedness is hard to credit,
And condemnation may be premature;
This way, I can be absolutely sure.
If what they say about this bet is true
I'd rather she were dead than married to
That monster! If my daughter's in his snare
Then death can take me, too, for all I care.
"Fine man" or not, he mustn't be allowed
To turn her bridal veil into a shroud.

Buttarelli returns with the mask.

BUTTARELLI: Your mask, sir.

GONZALO: How much longer will they be?

BUTTARELLI: If they *do* come, they'll be here presently:
At all events, they must turn up by eight –
The wager's lost if they're a minute late.

GONZALO: I pray to God these rumours *are* proved wrong,
And they were only joking all along.

BUTTARELLI: Well, God may grant that prayer, for all I know.
You'll soon find out. There isn't long to go.

Gonzalo sits and dons his mask.

BUTTARELLI: *(Aside)* What a mysterious old man he is!

GONZALO: *(Aside)* Reduced to waiting here and wearing this –
A man in my position! Nonetheless,
The welfare of my house, *her* happiness,
Demand it – nor am I prepared to let
Such matters be decided by a bet.

Enter Don Diego, masked.

DIEGO: This is the place – my sources were quite clear:
"Look for the laurel sign," they said – it's here.

BUTTARELLI: *(Aside)* Another mask!

DIEGO: Is this the Laurel Inn?

BUTTARELLI: It is.

DIEGO: And where's the landlord?

BUTTARELLI: Here. Come in.
Sit yourself down.

DIEGO: Don Juan Tenorio
Has an appointment here tonight . . .

BUTTARELLI: I know.

DIEGO: And has he kept it yet?

BUTTARELLI: Not yet.

DIEGO: I see.
D'you think he will?

BUTTARELLI: It's no use asking me.

DIEGO: But you're expecting him?

BUTTARELLI: It all depends.

DIEGO: *(Losing patience.)* On what?

BUTTARELLI: On what the man himself intends.

DIEGO: You're most informative. Let's wait and see.

      Sits.

BUTTARELLI: Refreshment?

DIEGO: No. Take this.

      He hands him a coin.

BUTTARELLI: Excellency!

      Bows, as before.

DIEGO: Now leave me.

BUTTARELLI: *(Aside)* He's a tetchy so-and-so!

DIEGO: *(Aside)* I never thought I'd have to stoop this low:
The lengths we fathers go to for our sons!
I mean to see it for myself, just once –
This "monster" I must blush to call my own.

      *Meanwhile Buttarelli is pottering about, laying tables
      and eyeing his guests suspiciously.*

BUTTARELLI: *(Aside)*
No food! No drink! What are they made of? stone!
It seems they come here to be left alone!
If everyone paid double to sit down
I'd be the richest inn-keeper in town!

      Enter Centellas, Avellaneda and two friends.

AVELLANEDA: They'll keep to it, alright. They'll both appear.

CENTELLAS: Then let's go in. *(Calls)* Cristofano!

BUTTARELLI: You here,
Captain Centellas?

CENTELLAS: There's an escapade
In prospect: wildness is my stock-in-trade.

BUTTARELLI: You're quite the stranger, though.

CENTELLAS: I've been at war –
In Tunis, fighting for the Emperor.
But I've returned to manage my estate.
More to the point, tonight at any rate,
Assuming what I've just been told is true,
I have an old acquaintance to renew –
So, fetch some bottles up, and while we drink
Perhaps you'd like to tell us what you think
About this wager business.

BUTTARELLI: First things first,
Since bottles quench a more important thirst
Than news!

*He goes out, not without a contemptuous glance at the
old teetotallers.*

CENTELLAS: Let's sit.
(They seat themselves round a table.)
                                                        Avellaneda here
Can tell us more of Don Luis.

AVELLANEDA: I fear
I've told you all there is to tell. Of course
The harm he's done is certain to be worse
Than Juan Tenorio's. My money's on
Mejia.

CENTELLAS: Then you're backing the wrong don!
For evil on a truly global scale
Tenorio's unequalled – *he* won't fail:
His sins are effortless, and if he tries . . .
Well, it's impossible to visualise!
His lawlessness (and luck) are legendary –
I'll stake my fortune on him . . .

AVELLANEDA: That suits me!

*They shake on it – playfully, perhaps. Buttarelli
returns and places three bottles on the table.*

BUTTARELLI: There's Burgundy, Falernian, and Sorrento.

CENTELLAS: Pour us the best.

(Buttarelli pours during the following.)

                              What credence should we lend to
                    These rumours that Tenorio and Mejia
                    Have had a wager on for the past year?

BUTTARELLI: I'm not sure, but I'll tell you what I know.

CENTELLAS/
AVELLANEDA: Speak!

BUTTARELLI: To be honest with you, even though
                    They made the wager in this very inn,
                    I thought it wouldn't come to anything.
                    A year is such a long time. Anyhow,
                    The whole affair had slipped my mind till now:
                    About an hour ago, in walked this man –
                    Demanded ink and paper and began
                    A letter. What a letter! Fast and furious
                    The words were whizzing off his pen! Being curious,
                    I tried to pump his servant – learned that he's
                    A countryman of mine – a Genoese –
                    But that was all the fellow would reveal –
                    It was a bit like questioning an eel.
                    Meanwhile, his master put away his pen –
                    Gave him the letter to deliver – then
                    Asked me for news of Don Luis, although
                    He said the wager with Tenorio
                    Was ancient history – and he also knew
                    That one of them would keep the rendez-vous.
                    "Do you know something I don't know?" I said.
                    He wasn't telling – gave me these instead –
                    (Shows the coins.)
                    With this instruction, as a parting shot –
                    To fetch two bottles up, the best I'd got –
                    In case they both arrived. The table's set –
                    The one they sat at when they made the bet –
                    Two chairs, two cups, two bottles . . .

AVELLANEDA: That's the man
                    All over! Don Luis!

CENTELLAS: You mean Don Juan!

AVELLANEDA: Didn't you recognise him?

BUTTARELLI: How could I?
                    He wore a mask. I had a damn good try . . .

CENTELLAS: But surely there are other ways to place
            The man you're talking to, besides his face.

AVELLANEDA: His manner, for example . . .

BUTTARELLI: I admit –
            I wasn't smart enough to notice it.

AVELLANEDA: But what about. . . ?

BUTTARELLI: Sshh!

AVELLANEDA: Eh?

            The clock is striking.

BUTTARELLI: It's striking eight!

            *As the clock is striking eight, sundry people enter. The
            dialogue continues. On the final stroke, Don Juan,
            masked, approaches the table that Buttarelli has set,
            centre stage, and is about to occupy one of the chairs
            before it. He is closely followed by Don Luis, also
            masked, who makes for the other chair. Their servants
            (Ciutti, Gaston.) with them. All watch.*

AVELLANEDA: The audience has begun to congregate.

CENTELLAS: News of the wager's spread throughout Seville.

AVELLANEDA: If they turn up he'll get a shock, he will!

            Pointing at Don Juan.

CENTELLAS: The same goes for that other fellow there.

            Pointing at Don Luis.

DON JUAN: That chair's reserved.

LUIS: So's that one.

DON JUAN: No. This chair
            Is definitely mine.

LUIS: And this one here
            Is mine.

DON JUAN: You must be Don Luis Mejia.

LUIS: And you must be Don Juan Tenorio.

DON JUAN: Perhaps.

LUIS: *(Sceptical)* I see.

DON JUAN: You don't believe me?

LUIS: No.

DON JUAN: Nor I you.

LUIS: Don't let's fool about like this:

DON JUAN: Alright then, I'm Don Juan.

He removes his mask.

LUIS: I'm Don Luis.

He does likewise. They sit and remove their hats. Centellas, Avellaneda, Buttarelli and sundry others now come forward and greet them. Friendly gestures abound.

CENTELLAS: Don Juan!

AVELLANEDA: Don Luis!

DON JUAN: Comrades!

LUIS: Friends! Delighted
To see you here.

AVELLANEDA: I know we weren't invited,
But, having heard about this bet of yours,
We thought we'd come and see . . .

LUIS: Why not?

DON JUAN: Of course.
But let's waste no more time – pull up your chairs.

LUIS: And I suppose they'd better pull up theirs.

He indicates the others.

DON JUAN: *(To others.)* You're welcome, gentlemen. In fact, we're flattered.
We'd no idea how much this wager mattered!

LUIS: He's right. This is a man to man affair,
Of course, but why the Devil should we care
Who knows about it?

DON JUAN: Care?! To Hell with it!
Nobody's calling *me* a hypocrite!

I'm a good sinner – everywhere I go,
My wickedness goes too – isn't that so?

LUIS: Ha!
                (He turns to Don Gonzalo and Don Diego.)
                        What about you two? Come on – draw near:
                Why *over*hear what you can simply hear?

DIEGO: I'm happy where I am.

LUIS: And you?

GONZALO: I'm close
                Enough.

LUIS: They have their reasons, I suppose.

DON JUAN: Now – are we ready?

LUIS: Yes.

DON JUAN: Then I'd've thought
                It's time each man delivered his report.

LUIS: I'd like a drink before we start.

DON JUAN: Me too!

                *(Buttarelli pours for them, and they take long, hard
                swigs.)*

                Now then – the bet . . .

LUIS: *(To the assembled company.)* Let me recap for you:
                One day, I made so bold as to maintain
                That no one, through the length and breadth of Spain,
                Could match my deeds . . .

DON JUAN: . . . and since I felt the same
                About my own, I made a counterclaim . . .

LUIS: . . . which soon resulted in a bet – to see
                Who could inflict more harm more easily
                In one full year.

DON JUAN: Alright, let's hear the worst.

LUIS: You made the counterclaim, so you go first.

DON JUAN: I'll gladly do so, if you'd rather wait –
                It's not my custom to prevaricate.
                It seemed to me, I couldn't give full rein

To my peculiar talents here in Spain –
Italy was the land I headed for –
A place synonymous with Love and War
Since ancient times. We were campaigning there
Against the French and the Italians! Where
Could opportunities to overreach,
Or hairbreadth 'scapes i' the imminent deadly breach
Be more abundant? It's a well-known fact:
Encampments are invariably packed
With brawlers, gamesters and lotharios . . .
This, comrades, was the stamping ground I chose.
In Rome, to meet my new found obligation,
By way of challenge, or of invitation,
Depending on the reader's preferences,
I put a notice up – it read like this:
"This is Tenorio's house – apply within
For all varieties of vice and sin;
Any suggestions gratefully received
From gamblers, women, murderers and thieves."
I won't go into detail – let's just say
I made my mark before I came away.
The Roman girls, with their licentious ways –
The moral climate of the place these days!
Myself, so handsome and so debonnaire –
I wouldn't like to count my conquests there!
In view of this, you'll hardly be surprised
To learn I had to flee from Rome disguised
In rags, and mounted on a clapped out jade –
In fact, they would have hanged me if I'd stayed.
I joined the Spanish army, whereupon
I killed six men in duels and hurried on
To Naples – that terrestrial paradise –
A sort of vast emporium of vice –
Where, once again, I chose to advertise:
"This residence is Juan Tenorio's –
The greatest ladies' man that ever was:
Fishwives in rags, magnificent princesses,
He favours equally with his caresses;
He'll also join in any escapade,
Providing there's some money to be made;
Just name your vice – he's master of them all;
For love, or death, Tenorio's on call!"
That's how it read, and in my six months there

I proved myself a swine extraordinaire:
In every *cause célèbre* I played my part;
Raised treachery and mayhem to an art;
Ground reason, virtue, justice, underfoot –
And broke a lot of female hearts, to boot!
I swooped on cottages, scaled palace walls –
I plundered convents, too – and in them all
Left nothing but dishonour and distress,
And bitter memories of my caress.
Respecting neither person, time, nor place,
Sacred and secular, noble and base
I scorned alike. I challenged men at whim,
And if one challenged me, I dealt with him –
For murder's always been my favourite sport –
My death I never gave a second thought.
Here – I've recorded all the things I've done –
(Shows him a long scroll.)
And I'll maintain the truth of every one.

LUIS: *(Dry)* I'm sure we're all enthralled. Please – read it out.

DON JUAN: Not yet – I think it's time you spoke about
Your own achievements. Were they as bizarre,
As bold as mine?

LUIS: I hope so. Here they are.

He shows him a long(ish) scroll.

DON JUAN: Good: we'll compare these records, deed for deed,
When you've delivered your report.

LUIS: Agreed –
Though I suspect there isn't much to choose
Between the two.

DON JUAN: We'll judge from what ensues.

LUIS: Well, then: like you, I hoped for inspiration
From an exotic field of operation,
And soon decided there could be no land as
Fertile in opportunities as Flanders –
That breeding ground for territorial wars –
That hotbed of imbroglios and amours.
I hurried there. To start with, fortune frowned:
In less than one month, everything I owned
Was lost, and Flemings gave me a wide berth,

Seeing what I was (or rather, wasn't) worth.
But, being of a friendly cast of mind
I looked about for company – I joined
A group of bandaleros – things went well –
We roamed the country, plundering pell-mell –
Then, after numerous triumphs, off we went
To rob the bishop's palace down in Ghent.
That was a night, that was! His grace had gone
To the cathedral, for communion,
Leaving his coffers open to attack:
I shiver, even now, as I look back
On that stupendous haul! But human greed
Was all too quick to rear its ugly head:
Our captain tried to commandeer my share –
I challenged him, and beat him fair and square –
Three times I skewered him, like so much meat –
He fell, a bloody bundle, at my feet.
That showed the bandaleros what was what –
They voted me their captain, on the spot –
I vowed undying friendship, come what might . . .
Absconding with the loot the following night.
My quest for gold took me to Germany,
But there a Flemish friar spotted me
And gave my name to the authorities –
I was obliged to purchase my release.
I met that friar later, quite by chance –
Shot him . . .

DON JUAN: Of course.

LUIS: . . . and then set off for France.
On reaching Paris (what a city, eh!
The Naples of the North, as one might say.)
I also advertised, like this: "My name
Is Don Luis, and evil is my game:
Je suis prêt pour les femmes, et pour les hommes –
I handle both my weapons with aplomb!
Come one, *come* all!" And in my six months there
I proved myself a swine extraordinaire;
In every *cause célèbre* I played my part –
Raised treachery and mayhem to an art –
I won't go into detail, let's just say
I made my mark before I came away;
Ground, reason, virtue, justice, underfoot –

And broke a lot of female hearts, to boot.
I spent my fortune three times over, and
To build it up again, I've sought the hand
Of a certain Dona Ana de Pantoja,
A wealthy heiress from these parts – my offer
Has been accepted, and the wedding day
Fixed for tomorrow. (I need hardly say
You're very welcome.) All the things I've done
Are listed here – I'll vouch for every one.

DON JUAN: There *isn't* much to choose between our tales –
Just as you said, they teeter in the scales:
Which makes it all the more important, now,
To be exact.

LUIS: Quite so. Look, this is how
I've set them out: one column for the duels,
One for the conquests.

DON JUAN: Those are just the rules
That I've been following: on this side, the dead;
On this, the numerous girls I took to bed!

TOGETHER: We'll count.

They swap papers.

DON JUAN: Beginning with the dead . . . let's see . . .
I make your final tally twenty-three.

LUIS: And yours . . . heavens above! It's thirty-two!

DON JUAN: I'm nine ahead.

LUIS: Let's see what you can do
With girls . . .

Tense pause for counting.

DON JUAN: Your tally's fifty-six.

LUIS: And yours . . .
Seventy-two!

DON JUAN: I win, then, on both scores.

LUIS: It's quite incredible! *Seventy-two!*

DON JUAN: The list includes the names of people who
If questioned can, between them, guarantee
Its accuracy.

He points to the paper, which Luis still holds.

LUIS: *(To others sourly.)* Thorough, isn't he?

Takes back his list and hands Juan his.

DON JUAN: Duchesses, dairy-maids – you'll find them here:
            My exploits covered every social sphere.

LUIS: It's hard to fault . . .

DON JUAN: Impossible.

LUIS: Not quite . . .

DON JUAN: Oh? Tell me what you had in mind . . .

LUIS: Alright:
            A novice, just about to take her vows,
            Would, so to speak, have made it a full house!

DON JUAN: I'll do it! And I'll add the future spouse
            Of an old friend . . .

LUIS: Well! What an appetite!

DON JUAN: Let's make another wager of it.

LUIS: Right.
            Double or quits. I'll give you – twenty days?

DON JUAN: I shan't need more than six.

LUIS: What? I'm amazed!
            Don Juan, are you a monster – or a fool?
            How long does each one take you, as a rule?

DON JUAN: You work it out: six dozen in a year –
            That's six a month.

LUIS: *(Calculates thickly.)* Yes – well – that seems quite clear.

DON JUAN: One day to woo her, one to consumate,
            One to get rid of her, two to locate
            The next one – and an hour or so, I find,
            To get the previous one out of my mind.

LUIS: *(More maths.)* Why *six* days, though, if you're
            attempting two?

DON JUAN: Because the first's about to marry you!

LUIS: WHAT DID YOU SAY?

DON JUAN: Exactly what you heard:
I'll do it, too, Luis – you have my word.

LUIS: Gaston! Come here!

DON JUAN: Ciutti! Come here!

GASTON/
CIUTTI: Senor!
*Don Juan/Luis whispers to Ciutti/Gaston, who scuttles
off.*

LUIS: Retract!

(Don Juan does not respond.)

Then it's your life we're playing for.

*Don Gonzalo now rises and confronts them.
Presumably, during what follows, he disguises his voice,
and Don Diego likewise. In fact I guess quite a lot of
voice disguising goes on throughout this play!*

GONZALO: Fools! If I wasn't weak and short of breath,
I'd take a club and beat you both to death
Like common criminals.

JUAN/LUIS: Try it!

GONZALO: Oh no –
I gave up hollow bragging years ago.

DON JUAN: Go home, old man.

GONZALO: I'll do so willingly,
But first, hear this: your father came to me
Proposing that, to end hostilities
Between us, and unite our families,
Ines and you should marry. But before
I could accept you as my son-in-law
I wanted first-hand knowledge, which is why
I came tonight, to watch . . .

DON JUAN: You mean to spy.

GONZALO: If you prefer. And frankly, what I've seen
Is unacceptable – absurd – obscene!

DON JUAN: Who is this doddering fool, and what's his game?

(Gonzalo removes his mask.)

It's Don Gonzalo, isn't it?

GONZALO: The same.
Forget this face – forget my daughter's, too:
I'll bury her before she marries you!

DON JUAN: Don't make me laugh! You senile lunatic!
Defy *me*? Bate a lion with a stick?
You'd better change your mind, for your own sake:
I'm warning you – what you withhold, I'll take.
I need a girl like her to win this bet –
I haven't had a little novice yet!

> *Don Diego rises, having sat motionless throughout the preceding.*

DIEGO: You *are* a monster! Those reports of you
That I refused to credit – they're all true!
Nor could there be a stronger proof than this
That the truth hurts, and ignorance is bliss!
But there's a thunderbolt up there, reserved
For your destruction.

DON JUAN: *(Dry)* Doubtless well deserved.

DIEGO: Since evil suits your temperament so well,
By all means, take the shortest route to Hell:
I wash my hands of you.

DON JUAN: What if you do?
I don't see why my future interests *you*.

DIEGO: Goodbye, then.

DON JUAN: Wait! I've something else to ask . . .

DIEGO: A favour?

DON JUAN: If you like. Take off that mask.

DIEGO: Never!

DON JUAN: Oh, no?

> *Don Juan grabs him and tears off the mask.*

ALL: Don Juan!

DIEGO: Insolent swine!

DON JUAN: Father!

DIEGO: What father? You're no son of mine.

DON JUAN: Go to Hell!

DIEGO: If I do, I'll see you there!
Gonzalo, can we keep what's happened here
A secret?

GONZALO: You can trust me.

DIEGO: Excellent!

GONZALO: Let's go, then.

DIEGO: Yes. We'll leave this recreant
To sin and solitude. Goodbye, Don Juan:
You've hurt me to the quick, and yet I can –
I *must* forgive you – God will judge.

DON JUAN: No doubt.
Meanwhile, forgiveness I can do without.
As for His judgement, it's a long way off
So don't upset yourself – I'm old enough
To handle my . . . affairs, and I intend
To live like this, right to the bitter end!

(The old men go out.)

The usual lecture! It's a family trait!
Now, Don Luis, I hope we've got this straight:
The old man's daughter, and your future wife –
Donas Ines and Ana . . .

LUIS: Or your life.

DON JUAN: Agreed.

LUIS: What are we waiting for?

DON JUAN: Let's go.

Enter constables.

CONSTABLE 1 : Which one of you is Juan Tenorio?

DON JUAN: I am.

CONSTABLE 1 : Then I arrest you.

DON JUAN: You're insane!

CONSTABLE 1: Oh, no I'm not!

LUIS: Perhaps I should explain . . .

DON JUAN: Do!

LUIS: Anyone can lose a wager, yes –
But to lose two might look like carelessness –
So I had Gaston here inform on you.

DON JUAN: *(Aside)* Intelligence! From him! That's something new!

LUIS: I win this time, then.

DON JUAN: So it would appear.

*He makes to go with the constables as more constables
enter.*

CONSTABLE 2: Which one of you is Don Luis Mejia?

LUIS: I am.

CONSTABLE 2:   Then I arrest you.

LUIS: You're insane!

CONSTABLE 2: Oh, no I'm not!

He glances at Juan.

DON JUAN: Perhaps I should explain.
Well, anyone can win a wager, yes –
I had to win both – I could do no less.
So I had Ciutti here . . .

LUIS: Alright, alright!
If we both die, I'll still be satisfied!

DON JUAN: Let's go.
(To others.) The bet's begun in stalemate, friends,
But the important thing is how it ends!

*They go, as do sundry others after them, leaving
Avellaneda, Centellas, some maskers and onlookers.*

CENTELLAS: Incredible!

AVELLANEDA: Amazing!

TOGETHER: What a man!

Exchange looks.

AVELLANEDA: I meant Luis, of course.

CENTELLAS: And I meant Juan!

END OF ACT ONE

ACT TWO

DEXTERITY; DEVIOUSNESS

Outside Dona Ana's house, seen from a corner. The two walls forming the angle extend equally on either side, with a grille to the right and grille and door to the left. Don Luis, his face covered with a cloak, enters.

LUIS: So, here I am, at Dona Ana's door:
To tell her what's occurred – and what's in store.
This time my life, and honour, are at stake –
No holds are barred, no risk too great to take . . .
But someone's coming!

Enter Pascual.

PASCUAL: What a night! Arrested!

LUIS: *(Stage whisper.)* Pascual!

PASCUAL: It's quite a shock! I can't digest it!

LUIS: PASCUAL!

PASCUAL: My God! It's Don Luis Mejia!

LUIS: What's up with you?

PASCUAL: What are you doing here?
They said you'd been arrested.

LUIS: *(Momentarily playful.)* Is that so?
Look, have you heard of Juan Tenorio?
He has designs on Dona Ana's honour.

PASCUAL: On Dona Ana's honour! Has he won her?

LUIS: Not yet. You *are* familiar with him, then?

PASCUAL: He's one of Spain's most famous ladies' men.
You're both supposed to be in prison. Well!
Really! Some of the stories people tell!

LUIS: The stories were correct. I was in jail.
My cousin intervened and put up bail –
He *is* the royal treasurer – otherwise

I might have lost a treasure that I prize
Above my life . . .

PASCUAL: What's that?

LUIS: You're on my side?

PASCUAL: Of course! *(With great solemnity.)* Till death!

LUIS: Alright then, I'll confide
In you: this same Don Juan Tenorio
Is mad, and bad, and dangerous to know:
The two of us had made a bet – to see . . .

PASCUAL: . . . which one could do more harm more easily.

LUIS: He thrashed me. But I couldn't leave it there –
I criticised him – made a foolish dare,
Which he accepted: now he's set his sights
On Dona Ana, by tomorrow night!

PASCUAL: Well! Now he's talking!

LUIS: Talking? The *event*
Is what, between us, we must now prevent.

PASCUAL: I'm with you.

LUIS: What did I annoy him for?
If he wins this . . .

PASCUAL: Now come along, senor!
You can't be frightened of him?

LUIS: Frightened? Me!
Of course I'm not – and yet, there seems to be
Some evil genius, always at his side.

PASCUAL: We'll deal with it.

LUIS: I pray to God you're right.
Don Juan's a bold and brilliant adversary.

PASCUAL: What if he is? He's still no match for me!
One man from Aragon – that's all you need:
And I'm from Aragon, so you'll succeed.

LUIS: You've no idea how great the danger is.

PASCUAL: I've wriggled out of tighter spots than this.

LUIS: *(Brightens)* He hasn't got much time . . .

PASCUAL: Listen, senor:
            I've come across Tenorio's kind before:
            They're always sounding off about their "feats"
            In single-combat, or between the sheets –
            It comes to this: old men? they've thrashed a few,
            And beaten up a shopkeeper or two,
            But if a proper swordsman comes their way
            They soon find out that bragging doesn't pay.

LUIS: Are you implying. . . ?

PASCUAL: Oh, I don't mean you –
            You may be mad, but you're courageous, too.

LUIS: My escapades are legendary – Tenorio's,
            If anything, are even more notorious –
            He's cunning, too: my fears are justified –
            If anyone can wound me, or my pride,
            It's him.

PASCUAL: Perhaps, but he's in jail – you're here;
            And just as cunning – what've you to fear?

LUIS: In jail? What's that? An hour, and I was free . . .
            If I got out that quickly, so can he.
            But there's a way to make things watertight . . .

PASCUAL: What's that?

LUIS: By staying here myself tonight.

PASCUAL: And what price Dona Ana's honour, eh?

LUIS: Damn it! She's mine tomorrow anyway.

PASCUAL: But haven't I just offered my support?

LUIS: What use is that, with villains of this sort?
            I'll either stay the night, which would be best,
            Or barricade the street and risk arrest.

PASCUAL: I tell you, if you don't give up this plan
            You're . . .

LUIS: Out with it!

PASCUAL: . . . a stubborn, headstrong man!

LUIS: But, don't you see? It isn't just Don Juan
            I'm up against – female inconstancy

Is no less dangerous an enemy.
We're desperate men, Tenorio and I –
Ordinary codes of conduct don't apply.

PASCUAL: I've served this lady since she was so high . . .

LUIS: I know you have, and I assure you, I'll
Be a good husband to her. But, meanwhile . . .

PASCUAL: *(Relenting)* My room is more than big enough for two –
Look – if you're set on it, I'll share with you.
But don't let on . . .

LUIS: You have my word.

PASCUAL: All right.
And, to be safe, we'll both stay up tonight.
Wait till the master turns in.

LUIS: When's that?

PASCUAL: Ten.

LUIS: He could have had her twenty times by then!

PASCUAL: For pity's sake! What *do* you take her for?
My mistress is a lady, not a whore!
Now, look: you see that window, with the grille?
Be there at ten – give me a call – meanwhile
I'll make arrangements. Adios, senor.

             Goes.

LUIS: Adios . . . I've never felt this way before!
Some instinct, that I don't quite understand,
Tells me my darkest hour is now at hand!
This woman has bewitched me, God knows how –
I never cared for anyone till now!
Although, for wickedness, we're on a par –
For *luck*, Tenorio's ahead by far:
Hell's on his side, no matter what he does –
The Devil's with him everywhere he goes!
If I leave now, I'm done for – let Pascual
Think what he likes – this man's phenomenal!

             He goes to the window, right, and hsshts through it.

ANA: Who's there? It's you, Luis!

LUIS: Ana!

ANA: *(Playful)* I see!
                  Whispering at ladies' windows now, are we?

LUIS: I've never been so glad to see you . . .

ANA: Why?

LUIS: I'm caught up in a deadly rivalry –

ANA: What rivalry? For me? Haven't I shown
                  That I belong to you, and you alone?

LUIS: But you don't know this man . . .

ANA: Perhaps I don't.
                  I know myself, though. Rest assured, he won't
                  Get very far with me.

LUIS: Please understand:
                  I'm not afraid of him – not while this hand
                  Can hold a sword. And yet, the man combines
                  So many, awesome attributes – a lion's
                  Courage and strength, the wisdom of an owl,
                  A serpent's guile . . .

ANA: He sounds a curious fowl!
                  Go home to bed, Luis. Sleep easily.
                  This sort of animal is not for me!

LUIS: Then, by the love you say you hold so dear,
                  Permit me . . .

ANA: Softly – someone may be near . . .

                  *Luis draws closer and begins murmuring through the
                  grille, stage right. Meanwhile, Don Juan and Ciutti
                  enter, street, stage left.*

CIUTTI: Sir, you've the Devil's luck, and no mistake.

DON JUAN: It didn't take that gaoler long to make
                  The right decision. Have you got the key?

CIUTTI: I've brought it with me.

DON JUAN: Splendid! Give it me.

                  Ciutti hands it over.

CIUTTI: This only gets you through the garden gate –
                  You'll have to do some climbing I'm afraid –
                  That convent's like a prison.

DON JUAN: There's no letter?

CIUTTI: The nurse is on her way.

DON JUAN: That's even better.
                Now, what about the horses . . .

CIUTTI: Saddled and
                Ready.

DON JUAN: You brought the men?

CIUTTI: They're close at hand.

DON JUAN: Well done!
                (He pats him on the back.)
                        All good Sevillians are in bed –
                They think I'm safely locked away – instead
                I'm adding two more entries to my list!
                Ha! HA!

CIUTTI: Ssshh!

DON JUAN: EH?

CIUTTI: Be quiet, sir!

DON JUAN: What is it?

CIUTTI: Just by that window there – a man!

DON JUAN: You're right!
                We've an adventure on our hands tonight:
                I bet it's Don Luis.

CIUTTI: It can't be . . .

DON JUAN: Why?
                I got out pretty quickly, didn't I?

CIUTTI: But *he's* not *you*.

DON JUAN: That's true. I think I see
                A female at the window . . .

CIUTTI: *(With misplaced snobbery.)* Probably
                Some menial.

DON JUAN: Or Ana. I must take
                A closer look, since my bad name's at stake!
                Collect the others and surround the house –
                But do it stealthily . . .

CIUTTI: She's bound to close
            The window if we do.

DON JUAN: Exactly. When
            She does, you pounce . . .

CIUTTI: On *him*?

            (He indicates Luis.)

DON JUAN: Of course; and then
            I'll make my move.

CIUTTI: But what if he resists?

DON JUAN: Easy: you slice him into little bits!
            Now, hurry: victory depends on it.

            Ciutti hurries off. We "rejoin" Luis and Ana.

LUIS: Then you consent to it?

ANA: Of course I do:
            My happiness consists in pleasing you.

LUIS: May heaven bless you for it! I shall keep
            A vigil, with the angels, while you sleep.
            (Going) I won't be long.

ANA: I'll see you here at ten.
            And don't be late.

LUIS: Wait patiently till then.

ANA: I'll have a key.

LUIS: Once I'm inside with you,
            I'll face Tenorio – and an army, too!

            *(Ana closes the window, leaving Luis in the street. Don Juan
            now approaches.)*

            Who's there?

DON JUAN: I am. Whoever's there is there.

LUIS: Meaning. . . ?

DON JUAN: Exactly what it means.

LUIS: I'll tear
            Your tongue out for you. . . !

DON JUAN: Will you, now? *(Advances)* Give way!

LUIS:	*(Hand on sword.)* I'm standing guard . . .
DON JUAN:	Go ahead: make my day!
LUIS:	Ask courteously, at least . . .
DON JUAN:	Of whom?
LUIS:	Mejia.
DON JUAN:	Ha! GET THE HELL OUT OF MY WAY! D'you hear?
LUIS:	You know me, then?
DON JUAN:	Of course.
LUIS:	Do I know you?
DON JUAN:	Listen: this street's not wide enough for two.
LUIS:	I know that voice . . . Don Juan!
DON JUAN:	And I repeat: Will you vacate, or must I clear, the street?
LUIS:	You got away.
DON JUAN:	If you did, so can I What's more, you've lost the bet.
LUIS:	I don't see why.

Ciutti has crept up stealthily with his comrades, who now seize Luis.

DON JUAN:	You see now?
LUIS:	First one jackal – now a pack!
DON JUAN:	Gag him, and tie his hands behind his back. Then lock him up till dawn. Luis, I've won – Winning's what matters – not the way it's done!

(They carry Luis off. Don Juan, alone.)

DON JUAN:	A masterstroke! The sort of machination That makes for an atrocious reputation! Locked in my cellar, tearing out his hair, While I seduce his bride-to-be up there: What could be easier? – simply take his place In Dona Ana's innocent embrace . . . You'll say I'm cheating, but remember – he

Wasn't above playing a trick on me:
The only trouble was, I played it back.
His luck's run out – I'm ready to attack . . .
But first, it mightn't be a bad idea
To make an ally of her maid, Lucia:
It's best, where evil-doing is concerned,
To leave no stone, however small, unturned . . .
(Sees Brigida approaching.)
What have we here? A Woman! Let me see –
I'm taking two on – is there time for three?
(Consults watch.)

BRIGIDA: Don Juan. . . ?

DON JUAN: *(Aside)* The nurse! *(To her.)* Brigida! I must say,
I'd clean forgotten you were on your way.

BRIGIDA: Are you alone?

DON JUAN: The Devil's with me . . .

BRIGIDA: WHO??!!
Sweet Jesus!

She looks about her in terror.

DON JUAN: By the Devil, I mean you.

BRIGIDA: Well! You're a one to talk!

DON JUAN: You could do worse
Than serve the Devil, when he fills your purse . . .
(Possibly tempts her with money at this point, later giving it.)
Now, get it off that ample chest of yours:
What have you done for me?

BRIGIDA: Exactly what
Your servant told me to – the little sod!

DON JUAN: My note?

BRIGIDA: She's reading it.

DON JUAN: I hoped you might . . .
Prime her a little . . .

BRIGIDA: Oh, she's primed, alright!
Don't worry – she'll be putty in your hands.

DON JUAN: Was it that easy?

BRIGIDA: Look: she understands
           Nothing of life – she's like a lovely bird
           That's been imprisoned in its cage since birth –
           Hopping about – not having seen the sky
           It doesn't have the slightest urge to fly –
           Or show its feathers off to anyone,
           Not having seen them glitter in the sun.
           Poor little thing! She's barely seventeen;
           What would she know of love? She's never *been*
           Outside the convent . . . convent! Huh! Con*vict*
           Is what she is – her training's been that strict.
           The same old round, from one year to the next –
           Confession, chapel, prayers, some holy text
           Or other . . .

DON JUAN: Being cloistered and confined
           Isn't the best way to expand the mind!
           She's pretty, though. . . ?

BRIGIDA: An angel.

DON JUAN: Then she'll do.
           And so, you've . . .

BRIGIDA: Filled her head with thoughts of you.
           It's like I say – so far as she's concerned,
           You're just the thing for which she's always yearned –
           Unconsciously – if that's the word I want:
           Your witty, worldly, handsome, brave, galant –
           That's what I told her – I believed it, too!

DON JUAN: Well I should damn well hope so, since it's true!

BRIGIDA: Of course, I also had to tell some lies.

DON JUAN: Such as?

BRIGIDA: That you were suffering agonies
           Of love for her – that if the situation
           Went on, your life, or worse, your reputation
           Might be at risk – I even said you were
           Her father's choice! In short, I peppered her
           With such a host of clever arguments,
           She's set her heart on you – her innocence
           Is fading fast!

DON JUAN: You've stirred me to the core –
           I feel as though I'd never loved before!

And what began as nothing but a game
Is now a quest – from a mere spark, a flame
Has billowed up – a furnace in my heart!
What convent wall could keep us two apart?
I'd plumb the depths of Hell to find her, such is
My ardour – yes! and wrest her from the clutches
Of Satan! Lovely rose, untouched by dew –
No – not one drop has penetrated you!
In convent soil you'll wither by the hour –
Mine is the only bed for such a flower!

BRIGIDA: Well, here's a turn-up for the books! I mean –
            You're meant to be a heartless libertine!

DON JUAN: Ines is perfect – how can I be bad?
            I've found the soul I never thought I had!
            The nuns are sleeping?

BRIGIDA: Should be, by this time.

DON JUAN: What now?

BRIGIDA: As soon as compline starts to chime –
            You make your move – you're going to have to climb
            A wall or two – the rest of it should be
            Extremely easy – simply take the key
            I gave that servant, and unlock the gate –
            You'll find a narrow passage, leading straight
            To us.

DON JUAN: And once she's mine – to have and hold,
            I promise you, you'll get your weight in gold.

BRIGIDA: You may regret that, when you've heard my weight!

DON JUAN: You'd better go.

BRIGIDA: I'll stop off at the gate –
            Talk to the porter – put her off the scent.
            I'll see you later.

                Goes.

DON JUAN: *(Alone)* This is excellent!
            I've played some damn good hands, but in my view
            This one's the best yet!

            (Ciutti approaches through the gloom.)

                            Ciutti? Is that you?

Ciutti appears at his side.

CIUTTI: It is.

DON JUAN: What have you done with Don Luis?

CIUTTI: Tonight you can commit your sins in peace!

DON JUAN: Then let's turn our attentions to Lucia.

(Ciutti goes to the window, then beckons Juan over.)

DON JUAN: I'll take your place – assuming she appears.

CIUTTI: *(Indignant)* Of course she will – we've got a secret sign.

DON JUAN: I see! But let me do the talking.

CIUTTI: Fine.

*Ciutti calls at the window, whereupon Lucia appears
and, seeing Don Juan, jumps back instinctively.*

LUCIA: Who are you? What d'you want?

DON JUAN: I'd like to see
            Your mistress.

LUCIA: Well it's not her policy
            To talk to strangers at this time of night.

DON JUAN: I WANT TO SEE HER.

LUCIA: No. It can't be right.
            She's marrying . . .

DON JUAN: . . . tomorrow afternoon.

LUCIA: And she's already been unfaithful? Go on!
            You're Don Luis, disguised!

DON JUAN: Watch what you say!!
            She's his tomorrow – but she's mine today:
            Sufficient unto . . .

LUCIA: She's expecting you?

DON JUAN: Perhaps.

LUCIA: Then what am I supposed to do?

DON JUAN: What do you think, girl? Let me in, of course.

LUCIA: And what do I get out of it?

DON JUAN: This purse.

LUCIA: What's in it?

DON JUAN: Gold.

LUCIA: How much?

DON JUAN: A hundred – more.
              Surely enough to open any door. . . ?

LUCIA: You're rich?

DON JUAN: As Croesus.

LUCIA: What's your name?

DON JUAN: Don Juan.

LUCIA: As in Tenorio?!

DON JUAN: The very man.

LUCIA: By all the saints!!

DON JUAN: I'm getting tired of this –
              It's money: does it matter whose it is?

LUCIA:.   The door . . . it creaks . . .

DON JUAN: That shouldn't be a problem.

LUCIA: I don't know . . .

DON JUAN: See these hundred? Well – I'll double 'em!

LUCIA: You're on. I'll need some time . . .

DON JUAN: You've got till ten.

LUCIA: Where will you be?

DON JUAN: Here.

LUCIA: Right.

DON JUAN: I'll see you then.

LUCIA: And don't be late.

DON JUAN: I won't.

LUCIA: I'll have a key.

DON JUAN: I'll have another purse.

LUCIA: Promise?

DON JUAN: Trust me.

(She closes the window. Juan beckons Ciutti over.)

That's bribery for you – never fails.

CIUTTI: I know.
I think we'd better get a move on, though:
Experienced lothario or not,
Even for you, it's asking quite a lot
To ravish Ines and be here again
To ravish Ana, between now and ten!

They go.

END OF ACT TWO

ACT THREE

DESECRATION

The convent. Dona Ines' cell. Doors back and left.

ABBESS: I know it's for the best. And anyway
Your father wishes it – you must obey.
You're young and beautiful – but virtuous;
You've spent your whole life, almost, here with us:
To enter holy vows, no evidence
Of your commitment – acts of penitence,
Or other trials – are needed: how can one
Repent the wicked things one hasn't done?!
Renounce a world one's hardly even seen?
You see how blessed your situation's been!

INES: *(Unconvinced)* I do.

ABBESS: No earthly pleasures or emotions
Can haunt your dreams and trouble your devotions:
How happy is the novice who recalls
No bustling world beyond the convent walls –
A tender dove, obedient to command,
Fearlessly feeding from her master's hand –
A little garden bounds her wish and care,
Nor does she try the nets that keep her there,
Or gaze, with longing, at the upper air –
No: like a lily in God's loveliest glade,
Your petals opened here, and here they'll fade.
Such innocence, once lost, will not return –
Hold fast to it! But why so taciturn?
So sullen? This is not like you . . . Of course!
You're always lost without that nurse of yours . . .
I'll send her here – she should be back by now –
She went to see your father. Anyhow
It's time you were in bed – goodnight, my dear.

INES: Goodnight . . .
(Ines curtsies and the Abbess goes out.)
There's something happening! In here!
(Indicates bosom, or some such.)

All sorts of strange emotions seem to be
Fighting each other for control of me.
So many times I've heard her talk like this
About the calm, the discipline, the *bliss*
Of convent life – its sweet simplicity –
They seemed the summit of felicity –
But now they've lost their charm – the life she paints
Is still – and full of odious constraints.
Just now, when she announced the time was near,
My first reaction wasn't joy, but fear.
Quite suddenly, my pulse began to race –
I felt the colour draining from my face . . .

Brigida enters.

BRIGIDA: Evening!

INES: *(Reproachful)* You're late.

BRIGIDA: Let's close this door.

She goes to the door and closes it.

INES: *(Horrified)* You know
That convent rules forbid it!

BRIGIDA: *(Unimpressed)* Even so,
We need to talk, and not be overheard:
That book I brought . . .

INES: I haven't read a word.

BRIGIDA: *(Alarmed)* Why not?

INES: Because I've scarcely been alone.
The abbess came.

BRIGIDA: That interfering crone!

INES: Why is it so important, anyway?

BRIGIDA: Forget it. Poor Don Juan's all *I* can say.

INES: Don Juan! You mean the missal's from Don Juan?

(Nurse nods.)

Then I must send it back at once.

BRIGIDA: You can't!
It'll go near to killing him, you know.

INES: It will?

BRIGIDA: Of course.

INES: I'll keep it, then!

BRIGIDA: Bravo!

INES: It's such a pretty book . . .

           Picks it up.

BRIGIDA: Of course it is:
           (Meaningful) Men go to any lengths with gifts like this.

INES: Such lovely golden clasps . . . *(Undoing them.)*

BRIGIDA: Yes, aren't they sweet?

INES: Small for a missal, though – is it complete?
           *(She opens it and leafs through. Juan's letter falls to the
           ground. She stares at it in amazement (horror?) then
           stoops to pick it up.)*
           What's this?

BRIGIDA: A letter for you, I should hope.

INES: From him?

BRIGIDA: Well, who d'you think it's from – the pope?

INES: Good Heavens!

BRIGIDA: What's the matter?

INES: Nothing . . .

BRIGIDA: Oh?
           Enough to make you blush and shudder though!
           (Aside) She's hooked! *(To Ines.)* How are you feeling?
           Better?

INES: Yes . . .

BRIGIDA: It'll soon pass – a touch of dizziness.

INES: There's something in this paper – it feels hot!
           It's burning me. . . !

BRIGIDA: *(Aside)* Is she in love, or what?!
           Ines! I've never seen you take on so!
           You're trembling! What's upset you?

INES: I don't know.
           For some time now, I've felt a strange unease –
           My mind is full of vague anxieties,
           Like shadows, reeling in some crazy dance . . .

BRIGIDA: Is one of them Don Juan, by any chance?

INES: I don't know. Ever since I saw him, though,
           And you explained . . .

BRIGIDA: *(Eager)* Yes. . . ?

INES: Everywhere I go
           I'm haunted by his face – I contemplate it
           In idle moments . . .

BRIGIDA: *(Aside)* She's infatuated!

INES: I don't know how, but he exerts some kind
           Of . . . influence over my heart and mind –
           And whether I'm at mass, or in my cell,
           Don Juan is sure to be there with me . . .

BRIGIDA: Well!
           Looks like a classic case of *love* to me.

INES: Did you say love?

BRIGIDA: I did.

INES: It couldn't be!

           She heaves an amorous sigh.

BRIGIDA: Of course it is. That proves it, too – a sigh.
           Now, read it out. You're hestitating. Why?

INES: The more I look at it, the more I fear
           Its contents . . .

BRIGIDA: Nonsense! READ IT. Now! D'you hear?

INES: *(Reads)* "Ines, my soul's joy. . . ." Is this meant for me?

BRIGIDA: Of course. He's being "poetical", you see.

INES: "Oh, beauteous dove, deprived of liberty . . ."

BRIGIDA: *(Aside)* Jesus!

INES: Vouchsafe to cast your lovely eyes
           Over my faltering lines – do not despise

The passion – the sincerity – of one
Who wishes to be yours, and yours alone . . ."

BRIGIDA: Well! Such . . . humility! And clever, too!
I like the bit about the dove – don't you?

INES: I don't know what to think . . .

BRIGIDA: Don't think – read on.

INES: "Heaven will smile upon our union:
Our destinies demand it – acquiesce,
And we can share eternal happiness!
You must consent to it, since you're to blame:
You struck the spark that grew into a flame
That grew, in turn, into a conflagration –
A furnace – a volcano of pure passion,
In whose hot bowels, Prometheus-like, I lie . . ."

BRIGIDA: Hot bowels?!

*Ines shows her the line, then reads on, Juan's passion
vibrating in her own voice.*

INES: ". . . Oh, rescue me! Don't let me die!"

BRIGIDA: He's worked himself up into such a state,
It'll kill him if he goes on at this rate!

INES: I'm feeling faint . . .

BRIGIDA: Go on.

INES: "Soul of my soul –
The lodestone of my heart – the very pole
On which my world revolves – please, condescend . . ."

BRIGIDA: We've had enough of that. Get to the end!
(She grabs the paper from Ines and skims through it.)
Let's see, now: you're a pearl without its shell,
Lost in the weeds . . . you're like a crane, as well . . .

INES: A crane?

BRIGIDA: That's what it says: ". . . you're longing to,
And yet you dare not, soar into the blue . . .".
But here's the bit that matters . . . ". . . if you're tired
Of your captivity, since you've inspired
This passion, send for me . . ." He says he'll do
Anything – go to Hell and back – for you.

INES: You pour these words like poison in my ears,
             Filling my soul with deep and deadly fears!

BRIGIDA: Don Juan. . . ?

INES: "Don Juan!" A terrible refrain
             Whose syllables re-echo in my brain!
             His image haunts me, everywhere I go!
             He says our destinies are joined – if so,
             I tremble . . .

BRIGIDA: Silence! For the love of God!
             You hear that bell . . .

INES: *(Momentarily prosaic.)* Compline? There's nothing odd
             In that.

BRIGIDA: Don't say that name.

INES: Which name?

BRIGIDA: The one
             That's echoing in your brain, of course . . .

INES: . . . Don Juan?

             Brigida starts in alarm and looks about her.

BRIGIDA: He might . . . materialise.

INES: How can that be?
             (Amused, in spite of everything.)
             Is he a spirit?

BRIGIDA: No. He's got a key!

INES: Oh God!

BRIGIDA: Be quiet!

             Footsteps are heard approaching.

INES: Footsteps!

BRIGIDA: Drawing near . . .

             *(The compline bell, middle distant, continues striking.
             Now nine begins to chime.)*

             Listen to that! It's striking nine. He's here!

             Don Juan enters.

DON JUAN: Ines – my love!

INES: *(Distraught)* Are you a spirit, or
A phantom?!

DON JUAN: Neither.

INES: In God's name, withdraw!

*She faints. Don Juan catches her in his arms. She has
dropped the letter, which remains on the floor.*

DON JUAN: Excellent! This'll make it easier!

*(He makes for the door with the unconscious girl in his
arms.)*

Now, let's be off.

BRIGIDA: Where are you taking her?

DON JUAN: Away from here – I couldn't very well
Finish the business in a convent cell!
I might be . . . interrupted.

BRIGIDA: *(Aside)* It's obscene!
He's still the animal he's always been!

DON JUAN: Please hurry up. My men are at the gate.

BRIGIDA: I'm coming. *(Aside)* Decency will have to wait!

*They go. After a brief pause the abbess enters through
the other door.*

ABBESS: I heard voices. They seemed to come from here . . .
They've gone! I knew it was a bad idea
To let Ines stay up so late tonight.
I'd better keep an eye on them – they might
Stir up dissent among the novices!

*(She is just going when, to her consternation, the sister
porter enters.)*

What are *you* doing here?! Your office is
To keep the gate.

PORTER: There's someone in the lodge –
Some sort of big-wig – said he wouldn't budge
Until he'd talked to you – it seems his "powers"
Include entering convents at all hours!

ABBESS: What's his name?

PORTER: Don Gonzalo de Ulloa.

ABBESS: I see. I wonder if. . . . You'd better go and
                Fetch him. He's the commander of the Order
                Of Calatrava - Ines is his daughter.

                Don Gonzalo enters.

GONZALO: Forgive me, please, Mother Superior,
                For bursting in on you at this late hour -
                A liberty that I was forced to take:
                The honour of my family's at stake.
                I have - or rather, had - a jewel whose worth
                To me surpassed the rarest gem on earth . . .

ABBESS: Your daughter Ines?

GONZALO: A lubricious ape -
                A loathsome, lecherous, fiend in human shape . . .

ABBESS: Don Juan Tenorio?

GONZALO: The very same -
                Is out to ruin her - and *my* good name;
                To be revenged on me, you understand,
                For deeming him unworthy of her hand.
                His ally, as I've lately ascertained,
                Is Ines' nurse. Now, *she* must be detained -
                That's why I'm here. And you must also see
                That Ines takes her vows immediately.

ABBESS: The danger naturally seems great to you -
                Her father - but I have my honour, too:
                However fiendish this Don Juan may be,
                I promise you, your jewel is safe with me.

GONZALO: Of course - I trust you. But I haven't time
                For further talk. Forgive me, though, if I'm
                A trifle sceptical - and fetch that nurse:
                I need to question her, at once.

ABBESS: Of course.

                (To the porter, a touch of anxiety in her tone:)

                Find them and bring them here.

                The porter goes out.

GONZALO: You mean they're not
            In bed, at *this* hour?

ABBESS: *(Pause)* No.

GONZALO: Tenorio's plot!
            What's this? A letter? *(Picks it up.)* Look at that: HIS
            SEAL.
            "Ines, my soul's joy . . ." Read it. *(Hands it to her.)*
            Imbecile!
            You pray for her, to God, and while you pray
            The Devil comes and snatches her away!

                The porter re-enters.

PORTER: Oh, reverend mother! A catastrophe!
            A man! Climbing the garden wall . . .

GONZALO: You see!
            After them!

                Going.

PORTER: *(Looking at the Abbess.)* After who?

GONZALO: For pity's sake!
            It isn't just my daughter that's at stake!

                They hurry off, Gonzalo leading.

                END OF ACT THREE

ACT FOUR

HEAVEN'S GATE

Don Juan's estate, outside Seville. An upstairs room. Window rear, leading to balcony. Doors left and right.

Brigida and Ciutti.

BRIGIDA: What a night! What a man! Christ! If I'd known
What was in store, I'd've left well alone.
Oof! I can hardly walk! I'm one big ache.

CIUTTI: Hm. Giving you that horse was a mistake.

BRIGIDA: God knows how I stayed on! We went so fast . . .
I mean – the way those trees went hurtling past!
If the journey hadn't ended when it did,
I would've definitely flipped my lid!

CIUTTI: That ride was just an average escapade –
Things happen here that put it in the shade:
We're always close to death – it's how he wants us
To live. The girl, though – is she still unconscious?

BRIGIDA: I hope so, for her sake!

CIUTTI: That's very true:
She should be in his arms when she comes to.

BRIGIDA: I'm sure that man's got Satan on his side.

CIUTTI: Or else he's Wickedness personified.

BRIGIDA: He's gone too far this time.

CIUTTI: I don't see why:
He won. Things no one else would even try
He can accomplish – in his sleep.

BRIGIDA: But still –
A convent! In the centre of Seville!

CIUTTI: That's just his Luck – She grants his every whim,
And the word "failure" 's meaningless to him
As long as there's a danger of some sort

He plunges in without a second thought.
The thousand natural shocks that flesh is heir to
Have never troubled him – they wouldn't dare to!
Nothing, and nobody, defeats him – though
One day, the Devil might just have a go!

BRIGIDA: Why did he stay, and we go on ahead?

CIUTTI: Because he still had things to . . . put to bed
In town.

BRIGIDA: Travel arrangements?

CIUTTI: Who can tell?
He's travelling, alright – but where to? Hell?

BRIGIDA: *(Crosses herself.)* Don't talk like that!

CIUTTI: I'm simply facing facts:
He's not performing charitable acts,
And that's for certain! But we'll be alright,
As long as he gets safely home tonight.
Not far from here, a pirate-ship is moored –
It's bound for Italy, with us on board –
Goes like the wind, so once we're out of port
You needn't worry about getting caught.

Female noises off.

BRIGIDA: She's up!

CIUTTI: I'll leave you. His instructions were
That nobody but you should talk to her.

He goes. Ines enters.

INES: My goodness! What a host of dreams I've had!
What time is it? I think I'm going mad!
(She gazes about her, bewildered.)
Who brought me here?

BRIGIDA: Don Juan Tenorio.

INES: *(Resigned)* I might have known! At least you're with
me, though.

BRIGIDA: Come to the window. Everything you see
Is part of his estate. If you ask me,
That convent's just a pig-sty next to this!

Take a good look, girl – see how vast it is?
It's all yours now.

INES: What do you mean, all mine?

BRIGIDA: Listen: you're in the convent, around nine,
Reading a letter from Don Juan – a text
That's far from holy. Now, what happens next?
(Pause)
You don't remember?
(Ines shakes her head. Brigida gives the audience an arch look.)
                                    A huge fire broke out!
But you and me – we didn't think about
Escaping – we were totally consumed
By Don Juan's letter, and we both assumed
That what had made the two of us feel hot
Was curiosity, or passion, not
The fire! That what had made us short of breath
Was sheer excitement! We were close to death
When Don Juan rescued us – or rather, you –
Since that's the sort of thing men only do
For love – he was amazing! but, guess what?
When he appeared, you fainted on the spot!
It's natural, when a man has certain – charms.
Fortunately, he caught you in his arms
And carried you away, with me in tow:
WE OWE OUR LIVES TO JUAN TENORIO.
And after that – well, where were we to go?
You in a faint and me half choked? He said
That he'd be glad to give us each a bed –
I took him up on it – that's why we're here.

INES: And we must leave at once – that much is clear:
My father's house is where I ought to be –
Propriety demands it.

BRIGIDA: I agree.
The trouble is, we're several miles from home.
Look there . . . *(Pointing out of window.)*

INES: The river!

BRIGIDA: See how far we've come?

INES: Brigida – what exactly does this mean?

BRIGIDA: I'm sorry. . . ?

INES: Well, I've obviously been
             Deceived - I don't know how, or why, as yet -
             But I've been caught, and *you* have spread the net.
             I've never left the convent, and I know
             Little of "worldly" matters - even so,
             I am aware that honour can impose
             Certain constraints - to stay in Don Juan's house?!
             It's madness!

BRIGIDA: But he saved your life . . .

INES: Did he?
             What for? To put me through this agony?

BRIGIDA: You love him, though . . .

INES: I don't know. I'm confused . . .
             Just help me get away - before I lose
             My wits completely! It was you who brought
             That letter from Don Juan - was there some sort
             Of magic in it? Did you plan that, too?
             The day when I first saw him, it was *you*
             Who told me he was waiting, made me look
             Between the shutters; it was *you* that took
             Such pains to praise him to me, day and night -
             You wanted me to love him - at first sight!
             You claimed he had my father's blessing - *you*
             Described the torments he was going through:
             Very well, if I love him it's your doing,
             Not mine - and I can still escape my ruin!

             She makes to go. Rowing noises off.

BRIGIDA: Wait! What's that noise?

INES: A boat! Bound for Seville!
             Come on! Let's take it! If you don't, I will . . .

BRIGIDA: Wait! Listen to me! Neither of us can.

INES: Why not?

BRIGIDA: BECAUSE IT'S CARRYING DON JUAN!

INES: God give me strength!

BRIGIDA: *(Looking out.)* He's here. He's stepped ashore.

His men will take us home, dear – but before
They do, we'll say goodbye . . .

INES: Let's hurry, then –
He'll never lay a hand on me again!

BRIGIDA: *(Aside)* That's what she thinks! *(Aloud)* Come on . . .

CIUTTI: *(Off)* This way, sir.

DON JUAN: *(Off)* Lights!
What have we here? A pair of fly-by-nights!

BRIGIDA: *(Hurried explanation.)* Gonzalo must be looking for his
daughter,
What with the *fire* and all – I felt we ought to . . .

DON JUAN: What fire?
(He gets a speaking look from Brigida.)
                  Of course! The fire! In fact, I've just
Written to the Commander, and I trust
That what I've said will set his mind at rest.

INES: *(Still suspicious.)* What *did* you say?

DON JUAN: That you were in my care –
Quite safe, and breathing good, clean, country air
At last. So why should you be out of sorts?
Stay here – banish the convent from your thoughts.
Look at the moon – she shines more brightly here:
The air is pure, the skies are always clear!
See how the night itself seems to conspire
In my attempt to waken your desire:
The scent of wild flowers lingers on the breeze;
The south wind whispers in the olive trees;
The nightingale complains the whole night long,
Bathing the branches in her liquid song;
The fisherman, whose boat glides smoothly through
The water's tranquil surface – he sings, too,
As he awaits the day: all these conspire
In my attempt to waken your desire!
The flame of passion is already lit
And your responsive heart has nurtured it:
Although my words may give it extra force,
Those flashing eyes, those pearl-like tears, are yours!
I long to taste their sweetness! No – too late!
Your cheeks are burning – they evaporate!

All these are tell-tale symptoms that conspire
In my attempt to waken your desire!
Why would you listen, calmly, as you have,
Unless you cared for me? I am your slave!
The fortress of my heart would never fall –
I thought – but now it has, once and for all!

INES: I've never known such agony before!
It's killing me! For pity's sake, no more!
Fire in my heart and throbbing in my brain!
You say you love me, yet you cause me pain!
What secret potion have you given me,
To undermine a virgin's modesty?
What magic amulet do you possess
Whose force is drawing me to your caress?
Satan himself had charm – and beauty, too –
What he denied God, has he granted you?
Your power's too great – there's no resisting it –
My will is being eroded, bit by bit!
Look how the river's sucked into the sea –
Such is the influence you exert on me;
Your presence thrills me and destroys my reason;
Your eyes bewitch my soul – your breath is poison.
Be noble – show compassion: since I burn
With love, kill me! Or love me in return!

DON JUAN: Your words transform me! Now I realise
You're offering me the key to paradise!
This passion is not earthly, but divine
(A strange emotion in a heart like mine!)
Why do you speak of Satan? Don't you see?
This is God's work – he's reaching out to me
Through you! No feeble spark of passion, this,
Such as the merest breeze extinguishes,
But a great blaze – and yet, its flames won't hurt you:
I feel I'm even capable of virtue
For your sake! Starting with humility:
I'll supplicate your father – bend the knee –
It's you or death!

INES: *(Melting)* Yours for eternity!

DON JUAN: What was that noise? The dipping of an oar!
(He goes to the window and looks out.)
A boat's just landed – someone's stepped ashore –

Wearing a mask . . . Ines, although I'm loth
To lose you for a moment, you must both
Wait for me in your room.

INES: But how long for?

DON JUAN: Let's see – a quarter of an hour? No more.

INES: When will I see my father?

DON JUAN: Soon.

The women go. Ciutti enters.

CIUTTI: Senor:
There's somebody to see you.

DON JUAN: Who?

CIUTTI: God knows –
He says he's only willing to "disclose"
His name to you. He's masked – and obstinate:
He claims that what he's come about can't wait –
Matter of life and death – between you two.

DON JUAN: I see. But couldn't you extract some clue
To his identity?

CIUTTI: 'Fraid not. I'd say
He was in deadly earnest, from the way
He talks.

DON JUAN: Anyone with him?

CIUTTI: Just the men
Who rowed him over.

DON JUAN: Go and fetch him, then.
(Alone) I live my life at a horrendous pace!
Who is he? Better arm myself – in case . . .

*(He buckles on his sword and also takes two pistols that
he had placed on the table earlier. Ciutti enters,
leading Don Luis, wearing a half-mask, who waits for
him to go, which he does, on a sign from Don Juan.
The two men face each other in silence for a moment.)*

Good morning, friend . . .

He extends a hand, which Luis refuses.

LUIS: I'm not your friend.

DON JUAN:	I see.
	Well, speak your mind: what do you want with me?
LUIS:	I've come to kill you.
DON JUAN:	*(With a certain frivolity.)* Don Luis again!
LUIS:	*(Contemptuous)* The time has come. Let's settle this like men.
DON JUAN:	Because you lost the bet, we have to fight – That's what you're saying, isn't it?
LUIS:	That's right. We staked our lives . . .
DON JUAN:	Quite so, but it was I Who won the bet . . .
LUIS:	I don't intend to die Like a stuck pig!
DON JUAN:	What do you take me for? A slaughterman?
LUIS:	I know you better, or I wouldn't *be* here.
DON JUAN:	If we can't be friends, Tell me, at least, how I can make amends . . .
LUIS:	I'll be content – when one of us is dead! You took my place in Dona Ana's bed, And now you have the gall to say you've won – When I'd been locked away – when it was done In *my* name!
DON JUAN:	So? All's fair in love and war . . .
LUIS:	And which is this? I've never set much store By proverbs.
DON JUAN:	*(Amused)* Then you'll die for her? I'd say That was a touch too high a price to pay.
LUIS:	I loved that girl – but after what you've done She isn't fit for me, or anyone.
DON JUAN:	*(Pitying)* That wager was a foolish one to make.
LUIS:	I counted on your failing – my mistake. Prepare yourself. *(Hand on sword.)*

DON JUAN: It might be safer, though,
            To do it closer to the river . . .

LUIS: No.
            We do it here and now.

DON JUAN: And risk arrest?
            You have a boat?
            (Luis nods.)
                                    Then wouldn't it be best
            To fight down there? Whoever makes the kill
            's immediately taken to Seville . . .

            Pause, as Luis works this out.

LUIS: *(Aside)* He's right! *(Aloud)* Let's go, then . . .

            Enter Ciutti, alarmed.

CIUTTI: Save yourself, senor!

DON JUAN: *(Fed up.)* Now what's the matter?

CIUTTI: El Commendador –
            Complete with army!

DON JUAN: Let him in. But hold
            The others.

CIUTTI: Let him in?!

DON JUAN: Do as you're told!

            Exit Ciutti.

            Now, Don Luis, my courage is well known –
            You trust me – that, your coming here has shown:
            I always keep my word, as you'll soon find;
            Before I do, though, if you wouldn't mind
            Waiting a moment . . .

LUIS: You're courageous, yes –
            I'm not so sure about trustworthiness!

DON JUAN: The bet was in two parts – I'll have you know
            That I've won both of them . . .

LUIS: What?! In one go?
            The novice, just about to take her vows . . .

DON JUAN: That's right: I tracked one down – she's in this house.

Now, I've a few loose ends to tie up first:
(Ironic) Suppose we fought now, and I came off worst –
Poor old Gonzalo would have you to thank
For a wasted journey – and there *is* his rank
To be considered.

LUIS: Listen – if you're trying
To talk me round . . .

DON JUAN: Just what are you implying?
Control your thirst for vengeance, if you can,
Until I've finished with this gentleman.
In there . . .
(Gestures at a door.) We'll fight – I promise.

LUIS: All the same
I'd rather it was . . .

DON JUAN: In the Devil's name!
Do as I tell you, man, and get in there!
And just to prove to you I'm playing fair,
Feel free to listen in – to interrupt
Us even, if you feel you're being duped.

LUIS: That you can count on.

DON JUAN: Just remember this:
A little patience never went amiss.

> *He indicates the door yet again, and Luis finally goes
> out through it. Meanwhile Gonzalo's voice is heard
> outside.*

GONZALO: *(Off)* Where is he?

DON JUAN: Here he comes.

GONZALO: Where is the swine? *(Enters)*

DON JUAN: *(Kneeling)* I'm here, commander . . .

GONZALO: Kneeling, eh?

DON JUAN: Supine
If need be!

GONZALO: You could kneel a thousand times
And still not expiate one of your crimes.

DON JUAN: *(Aside)* Stubborn old fool! *(Aloud)* Just lend a patient
ear . . .

GONZALO: *(Waving the letter.)*
            Fine speeches can't erase what's written here.
            This ink is poison, specially designed
            To infiltrate an innocent virgin's mind!
            You sacrificed her to your bestial needs –
            You choked the garden of her soul with weeds –
            You fingered and besmirched my noble crest
            Like a tradesman putting cheap wares to the test –
            Are these the daring deeds you're famous for?
            Is this why people speak your name with awe?
            Are we supposed to call it courage, when
            You rape young girls, and grovel to old men?

DON JUAN: Commander, if you'd listen . . .

GONZALO: Save your breath:
            The honour of my house demands your death!

DON JUAN: Till now, I've never begged for anything –
            Not even from my father, or the king:
            You can imagine, since I'm now prostrate,
            That this must be a question of some weight . . .

GONZALO: Fear – of approaching vengeance – nothing more.

DON JUAN: Good God above! Hear me, Commander, or
            I shan't be answerable for what I do –
            My instincts will prevail – I'm warning you . . .

GONZALO: You're warning me!

DON JUAN: *(Calming himself.)* I love your daughter, sir,
            And I believe that God has chosen her
            To guide my steps – to help me win redress
            For sin, and tread the path of righteousness!
            Her innocence attracts me, not her face –
            Her spotless virtue, not her youthful grace:
            Where priests and justices could not prevail
            With images of Hell, and threats of jail,
            Ines has triumphed, forging good from evil –
            An ardent angel from a hardened devil!
            Only consider what you stand to gain:
            I'm wealthy, and the bravest man in Spain –
            Accept me now, and you can take my lands –
            I'll place myself entirely in your hands –
            I'll go to any lengths to prove my worth,
            Since what I'm asking for is Heaven on earth!

GONZALO: You make me sick! You've added a new vice
To your collection, have you? Cowardice!
No mire's too deep for you to wallow in,
If there's a chance that it'll save your skin?
Well, I dislike this latest style of yours:
I'd rather see you taking things by force.

DON JUAN: But isn't concord preferable to strife?

GONZALO: I'd rather have her murdered than your wife!
Send for the girl – or die in that position:
(He threatens to draw.)
There's no alternative – I never listen
To beggars!

DON JUAN: Then you're sending me to Hell:
If I lose her, I lose my soul as well . . .

GONZALO: What's that to me.

DON JUAN: I've begged you on my knees
Perhaps I'll try persuading you with these!

*He reveals the weapons at his belt. As he does so, Luis
bursts in.*

LUIS: *(Sarcastic)* Bravo, Don Juan!

DON JUAN: Not him again!

GONZALO: Who's this?

LUIS: A friend – and witness to *his* cowardice.
(To Juan.)
You're nothing but a thug! I know your kind:
The sort who always come up from behind,
And when the going gets a little tough
They bow and scrape! I think we've seen enough
Of Don Juan's bravery!

DON JUAN: Have you quite finished?

LUIS: I will have, just as soon as you've been punished:
He must avenge his daughter, I my bride –
Or else, there are the officers outside . . .

DON JUAN: I've had about as much as I can take:
The sacrifice I was prepared to make,
My humble protestations of good faith,
Have failed to move you – well, let's see if death

Can do the trick! My courage is in doubt
You say – well, now's your chance to test me out!

LUIS: Well said! And now's *your* chance to vindicate,
Your reputation – with your life's blood . . . *(Draws)*

DON JUAN: Wait!
Gonzalo, it was you who took away
My one chance of salvation – when the day
Of reckoning comes, you'd better put my case!

He shoots him.

GONZALO: Murderer!

Gonzalo dies. Juan draws and turns to face Luis.

DON JUAN: Now: let's try it face to face!

They fight. Juan runs him through.

LUIS: *(Prays)* Our Father . . .

DON JUAN: Fool! It's far too late for prayers.
(He rolls Luis over with his foot to make sure he's dead.)
Now to dispatch the gentlemen downstairs!

Ciutti is now heard at the foot of the balcony, off.

CIUTTI: Don Juan!

Juan goes to the balcony.

DON JUAN: What is it?

CIUTTI: Jump, sir! Save yourself!

Don Juan weighs it up and opts for escape.

DON JUAN: Coming. *(To audience.)* I called to God, and He was deaf:
Heaven shut its gates on Juan Tenorio –
Let Heaven answer for his deeds below!

*He jumps from the balcony. We hear the splash as he
lands in the river, and then the boat, rowing off at
speed. A banging at the doors of the house below.
Officers, soldiers, et al., enter shortly afterwards.*

1ST OFFICER: It came from here . . .

2ND OFFICER: There's gunsmoke in the air.

1ST OFFICER: A corpse!

2ND OFFICER: Another!

1ST OFFICER: Take a look through there.

*He indicates the door through which Ines and Brigida
went out earlier. The women emerge on to the stage
shortly afterwards, accompanied by soldiers who have
fetched them from their room. Ines, does not notice
her father's corpse at first, but the absence of Don Juan.*

INES: Don Juan . . . ?

1ST OFFICER: The old man's daughter . . .

2ND OFFICER: Yes – must be.

INES: Don Juan! Don Juan! Have you abandoned me?

1ST OFFICER: It's worse than that – he's killed your father.

INES: No!
           It can't be true! *(Seeing the corpse at last and cradling
           it in her arms.)*

2ND OFFICER: *(Looking out, back.)* A ship! Look – there they go . . .

1ST OFFICER: *(Going to balcony and looking.)*
           I know the captain – a Calabrian.

           He spits.

ALL: *(Bar Ines.)*
           Justice! For Ines!

INES: Not against Don Juan!

END OF PART ONE

PART TWO

ACT ONE

THE GHOST OF DONA INES

The mausoleum of the Don Diego Tenorio. The stage represents a splendid landscaped cemetery. In the foreground stand various carved tombs – those of Don Gonzalo, Dona Ines and Don Luis, each with a stone likeness atop it. Don Gonzalo's tomb is to the right – he is shown kneeling; Don Luis, left, also kneeling; Dona Ines, centre, upright. Further back, in perspective, are two more tombs. Finally, as the apex of the perspective, stands the raised tomb of Don Diego Tenorio. A wall, with niches and inscribed stones, surrounds the scene. There are two weeping willows on either side of Ines' tomb, set up so as to serve the demands of the action. There are also cypresses and all manner of flowers to be seen. The effect should not be mournful or sinister. The action takes place on a calm summer night, lit by a strong, unhindered moon. The Sculptor has finished putting up railings round Don Diego's tomb, and is preparing to leave.

SCULPTOR: That's that! I've finished Don Diego's tomb;
                What's more, I've done my damnedest to fulfil
                His wishes: he's been housed for Kingdom Come
                Just as he stipulated in his will!
                Well! After this, I can expect no end of
                Commissions from the great hidalgos, who,
                Quite naturally, require the sort of send-off
                Where nothing but a marble tomb will do.
                Tomorrow, at first light, I'll leave Seville:
                These products of my labour stay behind
                So that the people can admire my skill,
                And read the marble index of my mind.
                (Waxing increasingly portentous.)
                When generations yet unborn behold
                These splendid monuments, the present day,

And my abilities, will be extolled:
These will remain, though ages ebb away!
(He addresses the tombs.)
For you I toiled beneath the pitiless sun,
Till all my bones ached, and I swam in sweat:
You're my posterity – it's what you've done,
Not what you are, that people don't forget.

> *He is about to continue when Don Juan, entering,
> interrupts.*

DON JUAN: Good evening, friend.

SCULPTOR: *(Irritated, makes to go.)*
                It's been a gruelling day:
I'm sorry, but I must be on my way.

DON JUAN: I shan't detain you long, but please explain
One thing – it's years since I was last in Spain,
And now I find this spot completely changed.

SCULPTOR: Of course. The whole estate's been rearranged,
In deference to the owner's wishes . . .

DON JUAN: Oh?

SCULPTOR: It caused a stir – I'm not complaining, though.
It's made my name, in fact. There's quite a story
Behind it – if I wasn't in a hurry
I'd tell it.

DON JUAN: Can't you?

SCULPTOR: I suppose I can:
This estate once belonged to a great man . . .

DON JUAN: Don Diego Tenorio.

SCULPTOR: *(Surprised)* That's right!
This Don Diego had a son – a blight
On his good name – a lecher, brawler, thief,
Gambler and murderer. It's my belief,
If what they say about this renegade
's remotely true, that the arrangements made
In Don Diego's will were quite correct,
And set the record straight.

DON JUAN: In what respect?

SCULPTOR: Simply, that he bequeathed his whole estate
As a last resting place for those whose fate
Had been to fall foul of his butchering son.
Here they all are – well, nearly everyone!

A proud, expansive gesture indicates the statues.

DON JUAN: Are you the caretaker?

SCULPTOR: *(Hurt)* The sculptor!

DON JUAN: Oh.
And are they finished?

SCULPTOR: Yes – a month ago,
Or more. My final task was to erect
A set of iron railings, to protect
The tombs from what he called "the common herd"

DON JUAN: I'd say you'd done him proud – they're the last word
In – what? Marmoreal splendour?

SCULPTOR: *(Points at Diego's tomb.)* There he is.
I'm a great stickler for likenesses.

DON JUAN: I can see that.

SCULPTOR: I took a lot of trouble,
With these.

DON JUAN: I'm sure. They're indistinguishable
From the originals.

SCULPTOR: You knew them all?

DON JUAN: Quite well.

SCULPTOR: These kind of statues stand or fall
By likeness.

DON JUAN: Yours will definitely stand.

SCULPTOR: I'm happy with them. On the other hand,
I would have liked to place the murderer
Among them – to complete things, as it were.
I couldn't find a likeness of him though.
They say he was a friend.

DON JUAN: Tenorio?
That's understating it!

SCULPTOR: You've met him too?

DON JUAN: Quite the most evil man I ever knew!
             If old Gonzalo there could talk he might
             Defend him, though.

SCULPTOR: He paid the price, alright:
             His father cut him off without a penny.

DON JUAN: Money! As if he ever needed any!
             Tenorio's the luckiest man on earth:
             All the best stars were present at his birth.

SCULPTOR: It seems he's dead.

DON JUAN: That's rubbish. He's alive,
             And in Seville.

SCULPTOR: If so, he won't survive
             The public outcry.

DON JUAN: Pah! He doesn't give
             A **** about the public!

SCULPTOR: All the same
             He's bound to feel a certain sense of shame
             On finding what's become of his estate.

DON JUAN: I don't see why he should: he didn't hate
             These people when they were alive, and he's
             Likely to welcome them as effigies!

SCULPTOR: You think he'll come?

DON JUAN: Of course. And so would I:
             Where you were born is where you ought to die.
             This mausoleum was his worldly wealth –
             They can't begrudge him six feet for himself!

SCULPTOR: The will denies him access to it, though.

DON JUAN: Who's going to keep him out, I'd like to know.

             Indicates sword.

SCULPTOR: I can't believe he won't respect the dead . . .

DON JUAN: Look – once he gets a notion in his head
             He acts on it, no matter how profane:
             He'd dig this mausoleum up again

And build a palace on it. Who "respects"
People he once reduced to jibbering wrecks?

SCULPTOR: Has he no conscience?

DON JUAN: Definitely not.
He asked for God's forgiveness once, and got
So callous a response that, there and then,
He murdered, in cold blood, two innocent men.

SCULPTOR: Jesus! The man's a monster!

DON JUAN: All the same,
In my view, Heaven has to share the blame.

SCULPTOR: I'm not surprised they didn't want him there!

DON JUAN: The man's worth ten of you.

SCULPTOR: *(Aside)* He seems to care
Deeply about Don Juan! *(Aloud)* Listen, senor,
I'm in a hurry, as I said before –

DON JUAN: Go, then.

SCULPTOR: I must lock up . . .

DON JUAN: Forget it. Go!

SCULPTOR: This is a private place . . .

DON JUAN: I like it though.

SCULPTOR: *(Aside)* He must be mad!

            *Juan walks round the male statues, then addresses
            them.*

DON JUAN: Good evening, friends – it's me:
I'm back.

SCULPTOR: *(Aside)* Insane!

DON JUAN: Good God! What's this I see?
It can't be! Dona Ines! Is she. . . ?

SCULPTOR: Dead.
Completely lost the will to live, it's said –
After she'd been deserted by Don Juan.
I saw the corpse.

DON JUAN: Describe it, if you can.

SCULPTOR: She seemed, not so much dead, as in repose –
             The freshness and the colour of a rose
             Still in her cheeks, as though to mar that beauty
             Struck Death himself as an unpleasant duty.

DON JUAN: Or rather, that he hadn't dared to trace
             His crude and clumsy pattern on a face
             The angels envied.
             (Addressing the statue.)
                          What I wouldn't do
             To bring you back to life!
             (To Sculptor.)
                               You carved this, too?

SCULPTOR: I did them all.

DON JUAN: But she outshines the rest.
             (Trying to suppress his emotion.)
             That's quite a gift you have! I'm most impressed.
             Take this.

             Hands him a purse.

SCULPTOR: I couldn't . . .

DON JUAN: Please.

SCULPTOR: But what's it for?
             I've had my fee already.

DON JUAN: Well, here's more –
             You've earned it.

SCULPTOR: Talent is its own reward.

DON JUAN: But economics shouldn't be ignored!

             Sculptor gives in and takes the gold.

SCULPTOR: Now, let's be off – I must return the keys.

DON JUAN: I'll see to that.

             (He holds out his hand for the keys. Sculptor hesitates.)

                               Just give them to me, please.

SCULPTOR: If you at least . . .

DON JUAN: Don't trifle with me, man.
             Good God above! Will you deny Don Juan
             The right to watch over his ancestors?

*(Scuptor says nothing. but mouths, in astonishment, the words
"Don Juan".)*

The keys! Or else the next tomb will be yours!

Sculptor hands him the keys.

SCULPTOR: *(Aside)*
He looks as though he's in the mood to kill!
Why should I care? I've finished with Seville!

He exits hurriedly.

DON JUAN: *(Alone)* Clear air, unhindered moon, and solitude!
How often have I wasted nights like this
Deflowering some poor virgin I'd pursued,
Or murdering one of my enemies!
After so many years of decadence,
My jaded soul has been rivivified:
This dispensation is divine – I sense,
Not Satan, but an angel by my side!
(An unfamiliar familiar!)
Permit me now, you marble conterfeit
Of my belovéd, lifeless though you are,
To lay my grief a moment at your feet.
Ines, your image comforted me through
A thousand dangers – now I curse my fate
For killing all the joy I ever knew,
And pour out tears of penitence, too late!
Ever since my departure, I have yearned
For one thing only – your divine embrace;
Heaven denied me, and I have returned
To find this cold, hard marble in your place!
Sweet girl, whose innocence and youth I blighted –
Witness my suffering through those eyes of stone –
Now, at the close, let our two troths be plighted –
Let Death, who parted us, now make us one!
You were the instrument God chose to bring
Goodness into my life – is it your voice
I seem to hear, soothing my suffering?
Am I delirious? Should I rejoice?
Was what I heard just then your parting sigh,
As Heaven claimed my treasure for its own?
If God *is* up there, in that starry sky –
Describe my suffering – ask Him to look down
On poor Don Juan!

(He leans against the statue. While he remains in this position a mist rises up from the tomb, concealing the statue of Ines. When the mist disperses we see that the statue has disappeared and Don Juan starts out of his revery.)

This tomb seems to exert
A curious influence on me – a kind
Of lethargy . . . The statue's disappeared!
Was it some figment of my anguished mind?

The willows and flowers to the left of the tomb alter, revealing behind them the brilliantly lit figure of Dona Ines herself.

INES: Don Juan!

DON JUAN: Dona Ines! My love for you
Has cost my sanity – take my life, too!
If it's my turn, act now – don't mock my pain!
But are you there at all, or in my brain?

INES: Both! I exist for *you* – by God's decree
Imprisoned in this marble purgatory –
My statue.

DON JUAN: Why?

INES: I haggled at the doors
Of Paradise – offered my soul for yours;
And when God saw my pure and tender passion,
He pitied me, and granted one concession:
"This fiend you love – wait for him in your tomb,
Share with him in My Grace, or in his doom!
Kindness and love must touch his heart – if not,
Your soul is his, and yours his desperate lot."

DON JUAN: I'm dreaming!

INES: You can make the dream come true,
Or ruin both of us – it rests with you:
Tonight we'll find our final resting place –
Whether in Hell-fire, or Eternal Grace,
Is yours to choose – and as you make that choice,
I beg you, listen to the still, small voice
Of your awakening conscience – weigh things well,
For balanced in the scales are Heaven and Hell!

*Dona Ines disappears and all is as at the start of the
act, except for the absence of her statue. Juan remains
astounded.*

DON JUAN: *(Jocular)* It's not diminished – the effect I have
On women! I can raise them from the grave!
(Dismissive) No. A delusion. My imagination
Has rarely toyed with me in such a fashion!
Or are there nymphs, imprisoned in these trees?
Well, who'd've thought it – Spanish dryades!
And yet, however sceptically one reasons,
I must admit, I felt a kind of – presence . . .
Ines was here . . . Rubbish! A fantasy:
Dreams often show us what we long to see . . .
The statue, though – what explanation for it?
That was no vision – it was *here*: I saw it!
I touched it! *Paid* the sculptor! Now it's gone –
An empty pedestal – what's going on?!
Is there some Hellish gadfly in my brain,
Scourging my sins by driving me insane?
Visions deceive the eye, but not the ear:
Those doleful strains – I heard them, loud and clear;
The message was: my time is running out!
(He attempts to steady himself once more.)
I'm sinking fast! I must cling on to doubt –
The wreckage of my reason; exorcise
This ghostly product of my fantasies:
Rest, rest, perturbed spirit! Remnant of
My blighted hopes and my aborted love!
Let them disperse, like flotsam in a storm,
And never gather in that heavenly form
Again! What's this?! More madness? Can it be?
The statues – moving! Gazing down on me!

*(Sure enough, the statues have slowly moved, turning to
face Don Juan.)*

Yes! Yes! They've moved! And aren't their features
more
Clearly defined now than they were before?
So what! They can't scare me – alive or dead,
Tenorio's ready for them!
(Addressing the statues.)

                              Go ahead!

Lavish your scornful looks! I'm not afraid –
Tonight will see my greatest escapade –
A battle with the dead! Take my advice –
Stay there, or I shall have to kill you twice!

He draws, as Centellas and Avellaneda enter.

CENTELLAS: *(From rear.)* That sounded like Don Juan!

DON JUAN: *(To audience.)* Who's that? *(Turns)* Who's there?

AVELLANEDA: Can you see anyone?

CENTELLAS: I think so.

AVELLANEDA: Where?

DON JUAN: WHO'S THERE, I say?!

CENTELLAS: *(Coming forward.)* I don't believe my eyes?
          It IS!!

AVELLANEDA: Tenorio!

CENTELLAS/
AVELLANEDA: What a surprise!

DON JUAN: More ghosts! Away with you!

Threatens them with his sword.

CENTELLAS: No! Look again!
          What's all this nonsense? *We're* not ghosts – we're
          men!
          And friends of yours, so welcome back, Don Juan.
          You're trembling, though! Your face has gone quite . . .

AVELLANEDA: . . . wan?

DON JUAN: Trick of the light.

AVELLANEDA: *(Peering at him.)* Good Lord! You *do* look queer!

CENTELLAS: But what are all these statues doing here?

DON JUAN: We're in a mausoleum.

CENTELLAS: On whose land?

DON JUAN: Mine. As you see – plenty of friends on hand!

          *Gestures about him at the tombs, which Centellas and
          Avellaneda now inspect.*

CENTELLAS: We thought we heard you talking, though – with
            whom?

            (Juan gestures about him at the statues.)

            Still jeering at them? Even in the tomb!

DON JUAN: Of course not. I was paying my respects –
            It seems conversing with the dead affects
            The brain – I felt a sort of giddiness –
            It *was* quite disconcerting, I confess –
            The statues seemed to – well, to threaten me!

CENTELLAS: *(Highly amused.)*
            Scared of the dead? Don Juan? How *can* this be?

DON JUAN: The dead can't frighten me – not while I breathe
            And wear a sword. No – if a second death
            Is what they want, I'll give it them!

CENTELLAS: Well said!

DON JUAN: I got some foolish notion in my head,
            But now it's past . . . Such things do happen. . . .

AVELLANEDA: Quite.

DON JUAN: I'd like you both to dine with me tonight.
            Let's feast ourselves, and when you've had your fill
            I'll tell you why I'm back here in Seville.
            It's quite a story – will you come?

CENTELLAS/
AVELLANEDA: *(Eager)* WE WILL!

CENTELLAS: You're sure there's nothing we might . . . interrupt?
            Some girl, with whom you would have rather . . .

AVELLANEDA: . . . supped?

CENTELLAS: You must have something . . . cooking?

DON JUAN: Alas, no.

CENTELLAS: When did you get here, then?

DON JUAN: Two days ago.
            It's just us three – assuming none of these
            Would like to join us . . .

            Gesturing as before at the statues.

CENTELLAS: Let them rest in peace.

DON JUAN: So you're the one who fears the dead! Alright:
              Here's what I'm going to do. Since you made light
              Of my . . . alarm, just now, I'll prove you wrong . . .

AVELLANEDA: How?

DON JUAN: I'll invite these gentlemen along –
              Tonight, my friends, you're dining with the dead.
              If something ghastly happens, on your head
              Be it! You had the insolence to suggest
              That I might fear them! Put me to the test!

AVELLANEDA: Don Juan!

              *Juan addresses the statue of Gonzalo, which is closest to
              him.*

DON JUAN: You were the one I wronged the most:
              Perhaps I can appease you – as your host:
              I'm asking you to dine with me tonight –
              There'll be an extra place for you – alright?
              It may be difficult to leave your tomb
              Just now, but if you can I've ample room!
              Is there an afterlife? I'd love to know.
              Is there a world up there, and one below?
              Although I've been an atheist to date,
              I'm sure the question's open to debate.

AVELLANEDA: The man's insane!

CENTELLAS: Vintage Tenorio!

DON JUAN: Well, let's be off. *(To Statue.)* I'm counting on you,
              though!

              END OF ACT ONE

ACT TWO

THE STATUE OF DON GONZALO

A room in Don Juan's house. Two doors rear, left and right, to suit the action that follows. Another door, side, left. A window, right. Don Juan, Centellas and Avellaneda are discovered seated at a lavishly laid table, the table cloth caught up in places, with garlands of flowers etc. Don Juan is facing the audience, with Avellaneda on his left and Centellas on his right, with an empty chair facing him. Ciutti in attendance.

DON JUAN: So there you are – those are the salient facts:
The Emperor, hearing of the countless acts
Of courage I'd performed, espoused my cause:
He pardoned me – my exile from these shores
Was at an end, and here I am.

CENTELLAS: *(Looking about him.)* What's more,
You seem as grand now as you were before.

DON JUAN: Some men are born great.

CENTELLAS: Here's to your return.

(They drink.)

That's quite a story. But we've yet to learn
How, if you've just arrived, you come to be
Living in such apparent luxury . . .

DON JUAN: It didn't take me long to get this house:
Forced seller – knock-down price.

CENTELLAS: Fortuitous.

DON JUAN: Poor man: some female gave him a rough ride –
Got into debt, sold up, and promptly died!
The notary in charge of the affair
Smelled ready money, took it then and there,
Swindled the creditors, snaffled his fee,
And made the whole estate over to me!

AVELLANEDA: And what about the girl?

DON JUAN: She was pursued,
                        But got away.

CENTELLAS: Worth chasing?

DON JUAN: *(Mock censorious.)* Don't be crude!
                        But yes, it seems.

CENTELLAS: If they'd included her
                        Along with all the other furniture!

AVELLANEDA: Second-hand women! For Tenorio?
                        Furniture, yes – sleeping companions, no!

DON JUAN: This house will more than serve my modest ends:
                        A place to entertain in style; old friends
                        To share it with – what man could ask for more?
                        Some wine for the Commander.

            He signs to Ciutti and indicates the empty place.

CIUTTI: Si, senor.

AVELLANEDA: Don Juan! You can't be serious?

DON JUAN: Why not?
                        Nobody's going to say Don Juan forgot
                        His duties as a host!

CENTELLAS: Must be the drink!

DON JUAN: My dear Centellas, what would people think?
                        The guest of honour, with an empty glass?
                        That isn't hospitality – it's a farce!
                        If he can't make it I'll be most upset!
                        But I'm not giving up on him just yet –
                        No – if he's half as obdurate in death
                        As he was in life, he'll come.

AVELLANEDA: *(Sarcasm)* How could we doubt it?

CENTELLAS: Let's drink to him and say no more about it.

            (He stands and raises his glass. They do likewise.)
            To Don Gonzalo – may God rest his soul.

DON JUAN: That's too religious for my liking! Oh well,
                        If you insist . . .

            All three drink the toast. Knocking is heard off.

DON JUAN: *(To Ciutti.)* Go and see who that is.

CIUTTI: *(Peering out of window.)* There's no one.

DON JUAN: Fine.
               Some prankster. Shut it, then, and fetch more wine.

               (Ciutti is about to obey when the knocking resumes.)

               No, wait . . .

               *He clicks his fingers at Ciutti, indicating the window
               again. Ciutti repeats the performance.*

CIUTTI: I swear to you, there's no one there!

DON JUAN: You've got a pistol. Shoot them if they dare
               Do it again.

               (The knocking is repeated, a little nearer now.)

                            This is preposterous!

CIUTTI: It's not outside at all! IT'S IN THE HOUSE!

CENTELLAS: The house?!

AVELLANEDA: It's him!

               They both rise in terror.

DON JUAN: Relax, gentlemen, please!
               A moving statue is no match for these!

               He shows the pistols at his belt. More knocking, nearer.

CIUTTI: My God! It's in the ante-room!

DON JUAN: *(Claps hands in realisation.)* Of course!
               (To Avellaneda/Centellas.)
               Admit it: this is all some hoax of yours –
               You've set the whole thing up, and Ciutti here
               Must be in league with you . . .

CENTELLAS: Not so.

AVELLANEDA: I swear . . .

DON JUAN: God! What a half-wit you must take me for!

               More knocking, nearer.

CIUTTI: It's in the drawing room!

AVELLANEDA: There's something more
               To this than meets the eye . . .

DON JUAN: You're telling me!
So – Ciutti must have given you a key.
Not very frightening, this "ghost" of yours –
Not if it needs a key to get through doors!

(He gets up and bolts the doors, then returns to his place.)

There – let him smash his way in, if he can –
And if he shows his face, he's a dead man!

CIUTTI: *(Aside)* He may speak truer than he knows!

DON JUAN: Admit:
One of you must have had a hand in it . . .

Centellas and Avellaneda exchange looks, from which it is clear that neither of them had anything of the sort.

CENTELLAS: *(To Avellaneda.)*
He's right, though – it's a set-up of some kind.

AVELLANEDA: Thank God for that!

CENTELLAS: Don Juan, you've put my mind
At rest.

DON JUAN: You're trembling, though . . .

CENTELLAS: I am? Well – yes!
I *was* a bit . . . perturbed, I must confess.

DON JUAN: But you admit it's all your doing?

CENTELLAS: No.

AVELLANEDA: Nor mine.

DON JUAN: I'll see that they regret it, though,
Whoever it may be. And now, let's eat –
Don't stand there dithering! Resume your seats!

They sit and reach for more food.

CENTELLAS: And then we'll sort this out.

DON JUAN: All in good time.

(Juan pours wine for Centellas.)

Try this. It's vintage Burgundy.

CENTELLAS: *(Drinks)* Sublime!

DON JUAN: Don't gulp it down – you won't do justice to it!

AVELLANEDA:Justice, indeed! Hardly *your* strongest suit! *(Drinks)*

> *More knocking, this time on the actual door of the set,
> rear, right.*

DON JUAN: This joke is getting tedious, I'm afraid:

> *(To Ciutti, who stands aghast.)*

Well, don't just stand there – fetch another plate!

(More knocking, very loud now. Juan calls out.)

Hey! You out there! What's all the knocking for:
Why should a minor detail like a door
Trouble a ghost?

> *The statue of Don Gonzalo now enters, noiselessly, and
> without opening the door.*

CENTELLAS/
AVELLANEDA: My God!

CIUTTI: By all the saints!

DON JUAN: Can it be true?

AVELLANEDA/
CENTELLAS: I think I'm going to faint! *(They faint.)*

DON JUAN: It's him, alright!

STATUE: What are you marvelling at?
You asked me and I came – what's strange in that?

DON JUAN: It's the Commander's voice!

STATUE: Of course. I knew
You didn't really mean it . . .

DON JUAN: That's not true!
(He indicates the empty place.)
Sit down. And don't imagine I'm dismayed –
Surprised, admittedly – but not afraid.

STATUE: So you believe your eyes?

DON JUAN: I'm not quite sure . . .

STATUE: Feel that: it's marble – solid, cold and pure.

            He extends an arm.

DON JUAN: No thanks! Now, eat! You're welcome – if you're real;
            But if you're playing games with me, this meal
            Will be your last.
            (To the unconscious Avellaneda and Centellas.) Get up!

STATUE: Let them sleep on:
            They needn't be disturbed until I've gone –
            The clemency that Heaven has granted you
            Requires no other witness than us two.
            Almighty God Himself instructed me
            To accept your doubtful hospitality,
            In the belief that, in His name, I might
            Lead your corrupted reason to the light:
            There is a life beyond this earthly one;
            Your mortal race is very nearly run:
            Your spirit's straining to depart your flesh –
            Be warned! This is your last chance to reflect.
            Question your soul: if you're prepared to learn
            How far His mercy can extend, return
            This visit – come at midnight to my tomb
            And dine with *me*. You're frightened . . .

DON JUAN: No! I'll come!
            I've told you once – there's nothing I'm afraid of.
            Before you leave, though, let's see what you're made of!

            He takes his pistol and aims at Statue.

STATUE: Is there no end to your Infernal pride?
            Look: *this* is what I'm made of – stand aside
            The thickest walls, the strongest iron bars,
            All elements dissolve and let me pass . . .

            *He walks past the astonished Juan and out through the
            wall.*

DON JUAN: Well – that was him, alright – I'm positive:
            He goes through walls like water through a sieve!
            And yet, just now, I heard him clearly state
            That he was stone – can stone evaporate?
            No – it's another of these fits of mine;
            Or else the previous owner got his wine
            From a bad bin! But even if it were

What it purports to be – God's messenger:
How could a night of penitence begin
To make amends for thirty years of sin?
What an absurd idea! It just confirms
My doubts: "God" wouldn't bargain on such terms!
And what of Ines' role in this grand scheme?
She's not here now – it's all some sort of dream . . .

The wall becomes transparent, revealing the Ghost of Dona Ines.

GHOST: Don Juan! Take the Commander's words to heart!
             Keep faith with him, and we need never part:
             For, from tonight, the two of us shall lie
             Together in one tomb – till then, goodbye!

She disappears.

DON JUAN: No! Wait, Ines! Reality? Illusion?
             Help me distinguish them! End this confusion!
             Just prove to me that these aren't fantasies,
             And my tormented soul can rest in peace.
             Will phantoms mock me everywhere I go?
             Have I gone mad at last? I need to know!
             (Tries to calm himself. Notices Avellaneda and Centellas, still unconscious.)
             Unless they *are* involved, and merely played
             Unconscious, while their little masquerade
             Was being performed. If so, I'll make them pay.
             (To Avellaneda/Centellas.)
             Get up! That's enough fooling for one day!

CENTELLAS: What's going on?

AVELLANEDA: Where am I?

CENTELLAS: *(Sees Juan.)* Oh, it's you!

DON JUAN: *(Controlled rage.)* I have a bone to pick with you . . .

CENTELLAS: You do?

DON JUAN: You made a fool of me – IN MY OWN HOUSE:
             Such antics can be VERY DANGEROUS –
             As you're about to learn . . .

CENTELLAS: *(To Avellaneda, am/be-mused.)* What *can* he mean?

DON JUAN: Just tell me what you've heard – and what you've seen.

It's my belief you spied on me tonight,
Back in the graveyard – when I got that . . .

AVELLANEDA: *(A hint of malice now.)* Fright?

CENTELLAS: Why should we spy on you?

DON JUAN: Stop this pretence.

CENTELLAS: *(To Avellaneda, as before.)*
He simply isn't making any sense!

DON JUAN: Oh no? Can statues come to dinner, then?
And bandy words with us? And tell us when
Our time has come?

CENTELLAS: Ah! *Now* I understand . . .

DON JUAN: Of course you do! This whole charade was planned:
You can explain it now, CONVINCINGLY,
Or I can kill you – which is it to be?

CENTELLAS: I reckon *you've* been playing games with *us*:
Do you still hold to this ridiculous
Story of phantom dinner guests?

(Juan is silent, but boiling.)

                                                        All right:
This is what *I* think happened here tonight:
I wasn't drunk, yet I lost consciousness –
Something I've never done before – my guess
Is that the wine was drugged . . .

DON JUAN: *(Menacing)* You've said enough . . .

CENTELLAS: That invitation! It was all a bluff!
Bravado! You could never bring it off –
Nobody could – so rather than lose face
You drug us, and pretend it all took place.
A joke's a joke, Don Juan – but I'm afraid
You've taken it too far this time . . .

AVELLANEDA: Well said!

DON JUAN: You lie!

AVELLANEDA/
CENTELLAS: *You* lie!

DON JUAN: Retract!

AVELLANEDA/
CENTELLAS: No! *You* retract!

DON JUAN: You've seen my courage – I don't speak, I act.
            Why should I cheapen what I value most
            By trying to prove it with a hollow boast?
            I'd rather die . . .

CENTELLAS: You shall!

He draws, then Avellaneda, then Juan.

AVELLANEDA: But is this fair?
            Two against one. . . ?

DON JUAN: An ace against a pair
            Of jokers!

CENTELLAS: *(Coldly)* Very well . . .

DON JUAN: Let's step outside –
            The dining room's no place for homicide!

He leads them off.

END OF ACT TWO

ACT THREE

GOD'S MERCY, OR THE APOTHEOSIS OF LOVE

The mausoleum of the Tenorios, as in Act One, except that the statues of Ines and Gonzalo are absent.

Don Juan enters. His cloak is up over his face. He seems distracted.

DON JUAN: They came between the dragon and his wrath!
I was the candle, and they were the moth!
And since I've simply sacrificed them both
To my insanity, I abrogate
Responsibility. Let's call it fate!
They knew my Luck – my matchless swordsmanship:
Death was awaiting them, at the first slip!
(A chuckle of satisfaction quickly dies away.)
My life's a wasteland – my tormented mind
Whirls through it, like a leaf before the wind.
My movements, like my thoughts, are not my own –
My strength has ebbed away, and the Unknown
Has taken charge of me. I recognised
No power on earth but Courage – I despised
All notions of a world beyond – but now
I'm wavering! If there *were* no spirits, how
Could my once cool, and hard, and rational head
Re-echo with that ghostly marble tread?
Those footsteps are behind me everywhere . . .
No: some, mysterious force has drawn me here . . .

(He lifts his head to see that the statue of Don Gonzalo is not in place.)

What's this? Oh, God! THE STATUE ISN'T
THERE!
It's all a trick . . . designed to sap my will . . .
Hold fast, Don Juan, and be a sceptic still!
(He calms down and tries to weigh it up.)
Suppose these *are* illusions? In that case,
Eventually, they'll vanish without trace.

If not, there's nothing I can do – the odds
Are hopeless: my displeasure against God's!
But if it really is some sort of late
Bid for my soul, I *would* appreciate
A more direct approach! This makes no sense:
The statue promised me clear evidence –
Let's have it, then!

*(He knocks on the tomb, parodying a knock at the door:
"TUM TITTY TUM-TUM – TUM TUM!")*

               Gonzalo. . . ! Please come out:
This is your last chance to dispel my doubts!

*The tomb is now transformed into a grotesque parody
of the supper table in the previous scene. In place of
garlands, silverware, etc., we see snakes, bones, fire,
etc. On the table is a bowl of ashes, a flaming goblet
and an hourglass. At the same time, all the other tombs
open and disgorge skeletons, still in their shrouds.
Spectres and spirits fill the rear of the stage. They
seem to be raising their hands to Heaven in
supplication. The tomb of Dona Ines remains as before.
The Statue of Don Gonzalo stands before Juan.*

STATUE: I'm here, Tenorio – and here, as well,
All those who wish to see you sent to Hell,
Petitioning God for your damnation . . .

DON JUAN: No!

STATUE: What's this! Not terror – from Tenorio?
What's happened to that "cool, hard, rational head"?
What's happened to the man who mocked the dead?

Don Juan is gazing in horror at the spectres.

DON JUAN: My victims! Yes! THEY'RE REAL!

STATUE: It looks as
though
Your courage is deserting you . . .

DON JUAN: Not so!
Not so! My sanity! My sanity!

STATUE: This is the threshold of eternity:
Your dust and theirs are shortly to be mixed –

Yes, and your never-ending sentence fixed.
Send not to know for whom the bell tolls then:
It tolls for you – the most corrupt of men!

DON JUAN: What does this mean?

STATUE: What Ines told you – what
I warned you of myself – and you forgot.
Arrogant fool! I promised to repay
Your hospitality, so come this way!

He motions Juan to the table.

DON JUAN: What have we here? Fire? Ashes?

STATUE: Yes, my friend:
These, all of us must come to in the end.

DON JUAN: Ashes, perhaps – but where does fire come in?

STATUE: The fires of Hell, with which God scourges sin.

DON JUAN: There *was* a world beyond, then, all along:
(Hysterical humour now.)
Of all life's questions, I get that one wrong!
An awful truth – a truth that seals my fate;
That mocks me by convincing me too late!
The hour-glass, though. . . ?

STATUE: It's measuring your last
Moments on earth.

DON JUAN: I see! I'm fading fast!

STATUE: Another moment passes with each grain.

DON JUAN: You don't suppose They'd turn it round again?

STATUE: Does Death amuse you?

DON JUAN: I no longer care.
But if you want my view, it's most unfair:
What does God mean by showing off His power
To a life-long atheist at this late hour?!

STATUE: One moment of contrition will suffice –
You still have time . . .

DON JUAN: What ludicrous advice!
One moment, for the countless things I've done?
One prayer, for every sin under the sun?

STATUE: Try it, and see! You'd better hurry, though . . .

               (Bell, off.)

               Listen – the bell! There isn't long to go:
               Your grave's being dug, and mass is being said . . .

                    The sound of chanting, off. Torches pass across stage,
                    left. Possibly, we see grave-diggers in action, though
                    Zorrilla does not indicate this.

DON JUAN: I know that chant: The Service for the Dead!
               How could it possibly. . . ?

STATUE: You lost the fight:
               Centellas killed you, earlier tonight,
               Outside your own front door.

DON JUAN: *(Totally serious at last.)* The light of Faith,
               Was absent from my life, but now, in death,
               Its dazzling rays illuminate my crimes!
               These hands were steeped in blood a thousand times!
               How many have I wronged? I cannot tell . . .
               Their grisly ranks will usher me to Hell!
               In every *cause célèbre* I played my part;
               Raised treachery and mayhem to an art;
               Ground reason, virtue, justice, underfoot –
               And broke a lot of female hearts to boot!
               I swooped on cottages, scaled palace walls;
               I plundered convents, too, and in them all
               Left nothing but dishonour and distress,
               And bitter memories of my caress!
               And are you telling me that, even so,
               God will take pity on Tenorio?
               (To spectres.)
               But still you wait, in stubborn silence – please –
               I beg you, leave me – let me die in peace!
               (To statue.)
               What do they want from me?

STATUE: Your life. Your soul.
               My efforts to return you to the fold
               Have been in vain . . . Come – bid the world goodbye.

                    He extends a hand to Don Juan.

DON JUAN: So you're my friend, all of a sudden – why?

STATUE: I did you wrong – God has commanded me
            To be your comrade for Eternity.

DON JUAN: So be it.

            He gives the Statue his hand.

STATUE: Come Don Juan – the moment's past:
            You've lost your chance – you're going home at last!

DON JUAN: There's one grain left! One moment of contrition
            Can cleanse my sins and save me from perdition . . .

STATUE: It is too late: your name is on the roll. . . .

            *Juan struggles to break free. The Statue releases him,
            and he kneels, arms raised to Heaven.*

DON JUAN: Almighty God, have mercy on my soul!

            *The spectres et al, now joined by the other Statues,
            bear down on Juan. The tomb of Dona Ines opens, she
            appears and takes his arm.*

INES: I'm here, Don Juan. God has forgiven you!

DON JUAN: Heaven be praised!

INES: Go back – infernal crew!
            Back to your graves! The will of God is this:
            My suffering has redeemed him.

DON JUAN: Dear Ines!

INES: My soul for his – it was the only way.
            The Pure and Wise, alone, will comprehend
            How love redeemed Don Juan. Go back, I say!

            (The infernal crew return to their graves as instructed.)

            Cease, chants!

            (The chanting stops instantly.)

                        Bells, bring your tolling to an end!

            (The chiming stops.)

            Statues, back to your pedestals!

            (The statues obey.)

                                (To Juan.) Your sins
            Are purged, and your celestial life begins . . .

> *The flowers now open, releasing cherubs that surround*
> *Ines and Juan, showering them with flowers. To the*
> *sound of slow, delightful music, the entire stage is lit*
> *up by the dawn. The tomb of Ines disappears, to be*
> *replaced by a carpet of flowers, on which she falls.*

DON JUAN: Tomorrow, let the people of Seville
Describe, in horror, how Tenorio fell,
His victims' victim – how the dead can kill,
And how they dragged me with them down to Hell!
The truth is this: one moment will suffice
To cleanse a lifetime's sin – and this is why
For Purgatory, and thence for Paradise,
Don Juan is bound – GLORY TO GOD ON HIGH!

> *Don Juan falls at the feet of Dona Ines. Their souls*
> *issue from their mouths, in the form of dazzling*
> *flames, which rise up, to the accompaniment of the*
> *music.*

THE END